Vanderdecken

H. De Vere Stacpoole

Alpha Editions

This edition published in 2024

ISBN : 9789362929259

Design and Setting By
Alpha Editions
www.alphaedis.com
Email - info@alphaedis.com

As per information held with us this book is in Public Domain.
This book is a reproduction of an important historical work. Alpha Editions uses the best technology to reproduce historical work in the same manner it was first published to preserve its original nature. Any marks or number seen are left intentionally to preserve its true form.

Contents

CHAPTER I THE FLYING DUTCHMAN ....- 1 -
CHAPTER II THE PROPOSITION ....- 6 -
CHAPTER III THE PLAN ....- 10 -
CHAPTER IV TYREBUCK..- 13 -
CHAPTER V JAKE...- 18 -
CHAPTER VI JOE BARRETT..- 22 -
CHAPTER VII THE FIRING OF JAKE...........................- 27 -
CHAPTER VIII PUBLICITY..- 31 -
CHAPTER IX CANDON ....- 36 -
CHAPTER X THE RED BEARDED ONE......................- 38 -
CHAPTER XI NIGHT..- 43 -
CHAPTER XII OUT...- 49 -
CHAPTER XIII THE BAY OF WHALES ....- 52 -
CHAPTER XIV ST. NICOLAS ....- 55 -
CHAPTER XV WHAT THE CHINKS WERE DOING.........- 60 -
CHAPTER XVI EVIDENCE OF CONTRABAND ....- 65 -
CHAPTER XVII THE SURPRISE ....- 67 -
CHAPTER XVIII THE ATTACK......................................- 70 -
CHAPTER XIX A SEA FIGHT ....- 74 -
CHAPTER XX DOWN BELOW ....- 77 -
CHAPTER XXI TOMMIE..- 81 -
CHAPTER XXII A PROBLEM IN PSYCHOLOGY ....- 85 -
CHAPTER XXIII THE NEW CHUM................................- 89 -
CHAPTER XXIV THE FREIGHTER................................- 92 -
CHAPTER XXV THEY TURN THE CORNER ....- 99 -
CHAPTER XXVI THE BAY OF WHALES ....- 101 -

CHAPTER XXVII THE CONFESSION	- 106 -
CHAPTER XXVIII HANK	- 111 -
CHAPTER XXIX THE SAND	- 114 -
CHAPTER XXX STRANGERS ON THE BEACH	- 117 -
CHAPTER XXXI "TOMMIE'S GONE!"	- 120 -
CHAPTER XXXII THE RETURN OF CANDON	- 125 -
CHAPTER XXXIII GONE!	- 133 -
CHAPTER XXXIV JAKE	- 141 -
CHAPTER XXXV SANTANDER ROCK	- 148 -
CHAPTER XXXVI "CANDON"	- 152 -
CHAPTER XXXVII JAKE IS FIRED AGAIN	- 156 -
CHAPTER XXXVIII THE ANCHOR TAKES THE MUD	- 159 -
CHAPTER XXXIX VANDERDECKEN	- 166 -

CHAPTER I

THE FLYING DUTCHMAN

GEORGE DU CANE was writing a letter in the smoking room of the Bohemian Club, San Francisco.

George was an orphan with guardians. Twenty-four years and five months of age, his property would not be decontrolled for another seven months when, on his twenty-fifth birthday, he would find himself the actual possessor of something over two million, five hundred thousand dollars. Old Harley du Cane, George's father, had made his money speculating. He had no healthy business to leave to his son and no very healthy reputation. He had ruined thousands of men whom he had never seen and never heard of, he had escaped ruin countless times by the skin of his teeth, he had wrecked railways; his life was, if logic counts, a long disgrace, and in a perfect civilization he would have been hanged. All the same he was a most lovable old man, generous, warm-hearted, hot-tempered, high-coloured, beautifully dressed; always with a cigar in his mouth and a flower in his buttonhole, his hat tilted on one side and his hand in his pocket for any unfortunate.

Only for his great battle with Jay Gould, he might have died worth ten million. He reckoned that he died poor, and, dying, he tied up his property in the hands of two trustees, as I have hinted. "To keep you from the sharks, George."

George didn't bother. Wannamaker and Thelusson, the two trustees, gave him all the money he wanted and the world all the fun. A juvenile replica of old Harley on the outside, he was not unlike him on the in; he had something better than wealth, than good looks, even than health, a radium quality inherited from his father that kept him far younger than his years. When Harley du Cane died at the age of seventy-six from a surfeit of ice cream following the excitement of a base-ball match, Cazenove, the broker, reading out the news to his family said the reporters had got the age wrong, for Harley wasn't more than nine; and he was right. The Great Bear, to give him his name in the Stock Market, in many respects wasn't more than nine.

George, having finished his letter, touched an electric bell. A waiter approached.

"Waiter," said George, "bring me an—Oh, damn it!" Egg flip had been on his tongue and prohibition had risen in his mind. The waiter waited. He was used to orders like this of late. "Lemonade," said George.

He got up and moved to where some men were seated near one of the windows. Cyrus Reid, the poet; Carolus, the musician; Abrahams, the artist. A few months ago these three would have been fighting, no doubt, over the merits of Henri, Matisse or the possibilities of Cubist music. Today they were just talking about how dry they were and of the great drought that had struck San Francisco. Reid was mostly a coffee drinker, an occasional glass of beer satisfied Carolus, and Abrahams was all but teetotal, yet they were filled with discontent. George sat down with them and listened to them and drank his lemonade and absorbed their gloom. Prohibition may be good or it may be bad, but there is one undoubted fact about it, it doesn't improve the social life of a club. Whilst they were talking, Hank Fisher came in. Hank was twenty-three or so; thin, tanned, hollow-cheeked, he looked like the mixture of a red Indian and an East coast Yankee.

He had been born in New Hampshire, served in a whaler, driven an engine, waited in a café, hoboed, stoked a Stockton river boat, canned in a cannery. He had educated himself, in a wild sort of way that produced flowers of the mind in an extraordinary pattern; he was both a Socialist and an individualist. There was nothing that the hands of men could do that the hands of Hank couldn't. He could make boots or a fishing-net or mend a watch, he had invented and patented a rat trap that brought him in a small income, and he had the specifications in hand of a clock that would go for forty-eight years without winding. He had, also, in the last year or two, made quite a sum of money speculating in real estate. But the crowning point of Hank, and the thing that had secured his entry to the Bohemian Club and endeared him to all imaginative people, was the fact that he was a little bit mad. Not crazy mad, but pleasantly mad. A madness so mixed with cold sanity and streaks of genius that you could scarcely call it madness.

"You can't tell what he'll do next," was the best description of him, given by Cedarquist, barring Reid's "He's an opal."

The opal sat down with scarcely a word and listened to Abrahams, who was holding forth. Said Abrahams:

"Yes, sir, you may talk and talk, but you haven't got to the bed-rock of the subject. The fact is the world never struck universal unrest till it struck universal lime-juice. If you could dig up the Czar and make him talk, I'll bet he'd back me. Talk of crime waves, when has crime ever waved before as it's waving now? Look at the hold-ups, look at New York, look at Chicago, look at this town. Look at the things that are done in the broad light of day. Milligan's raided yesterday by two gunmen and the place cleared of fifty thousand dollars' worth of stuff in fifteen minutes. Look at this chap Vanderdecken."

"What's he been doing?" asked Carolus.

"Doing! Don't you read the papers?"

"No," said Carolus.

"Doing. Why this chap's been on the job for the last six months and there's twenty-five thousand dollars reward out for him. Yacht raiding, that's what he's been doing, down the coast. Holding up pleasure yachts, comes along in a high power motor boat sometimes and sometimes he uses a fishing boat and no one knows where he changes ship or how he does it or how many are working with him."

"Oh," said Carolus. "Well he's doing nothing new. If you were as old as I am, you'd remember Mullins, away back in the middle 'nineties, he used to do the same thing. Got caught and I forget what they gave him. There's nothing new under the sun."

"Well, they hadn't wireless in the middle 'nineties," said Abrahams, "and wireless doesn't hold Vanderdecken, he skips over it or gets under it. Dutch Pete is his real name, they say, but someone labeled him Vanderdecken from the 'Flying Dutchman'."

"I know all about the fellow," cut in Hank Fisher, "know him from his toe-nails up. He's precious small potatoes, too. Lord, what a lot of misinformation manages to get about. Dutch Pete wasn't his name to start with, either. Amsterdam Joe was his name. He came from Hamburg and started here loading grain at Brookland Creek, then he got loose on the front—in with McKay and that lot—managed a whisky joint and got in trouble over something or other, and squared it and got into the Fish Patrol and got fired for colluding with the Greeks in setting Chinese sturgeon lines. Then, after the war, he managed to get some sort of an old boat and cleared out of here. He's down south and I could put my finger on him if I wanted to. Shark fishing is what he started on and he's held up a two cent yacht or two, there's no doubt about that, but as for motor boats and Flying Dutchmen, that's all the newspaper talk. They've embroidered on him till he looks like a king. Dutch Pete was a different chap altogether, but he's not about now. I saw him shot. It was in a dust-up at San Leandro."

"Have you seen the papers this morning?" asked Abrahams.

"Nope."

"Well, Vanderdecken, or Amsterdam Joe, or whatever you call him, has held up the *Satanita* as she was coming up from Avalon. She's no two cent yacht, she's all of eight hundred tons. He went through her and skipped with ten thousand dollars' worth of stuff."

"Give us the yarn," said Hank.

"Oh, it was as easy as pie. Connart was coming up in the *Satanita*—got his wife with him too—and somewhere off St. Luis Obispo they sighted a yawl. She wasn't more than forty or fifty tons and was lying hove to with her flag half masted. They stopped the engines, like fools, and the yawl sent a boat on board. Two fellows came over the side. One fellow put an automatic pistol to Connart's head and the other man with another automatic covered the officer on the bridge. There was nothing on board the *Satanita* but a deck gun and a nickel plated revolver, so she was helpless. Then two more fellows came on board from the boat and went through her. They smashed up the wireless first. Then they skipped and that old broken-down looking yawl went off to the south under an auxiliary engine."

"And why the blazes didn't they chase and ram her?" asked Hank.

"Couldn't. The rudder was jammed. The fellows in the boat had done some tinkering work to it. It took them two days to get it right, and they can't even give a full description of the men, for they wore caps with slits in them. Pulled the caps over their faces as they came aboard and looked through the slits."

"I expect the Navy will take it in hand," said George du Cane. "A couple of destroyers will soon run them down wherever they are hidden."

Hank Fisher laughed. "You might as well go hunting for an honest man in Market Street with a couple of rat terriers," said Hank. "First, you wouldn't find him, second he wouldn't be a rat. Why, that auxiliary yawl is either at the bottom by now, or converted into something else—and the guys on board her, do you think they're traveling about the Pacific with their slit caps over their faces waiting for a destroyer to fetch them home? What did you say the reward was—twenty-five thousand? You wait one minute."

He rose up and left the room.

"What's the matter with Hank now?" asked George.

"Search me," replied Abrahams, "unless he's gone off to 'phone the police all about Vanderdecken being Amsterdam Joe and his description."

"He'd never do that," said Carolus. "He's too chivalrous; you fellows don't know Hank. I don't rightly know him myself. He's a contradiction, something as new as wireless and as old as Don Quixote, but the Don's there all the time. I saw him giving his arm to an old woman in Market Street the other day; looked like a washerwoman. She'd tumbled down and hurt her leg or something and there was Hank handing her like a duchess on to a car. He believes in the sanctity of womanhood—told me so once."

"And he believes in the rights of man," said Abrahams, "but he'd beat you out of your back teeth in one of his infernal land speculations."

"And then buy you a new set," said Carolus, "and swindle the dentist out of a commission on the deal. Not that he cares for money."

"Oh, no, he doesn't care for money," said Abrahams. "I'll admit that, but he's a pirate all the same. It's his romantic temperament, maybe, mixed up with his New England ancestry. Here he is."

"Boys," said Hank, as he approached the group, "it's true enough, I've been on the 'phone; there's twenty-five thousand dollars reward out for the Dutchman, half put up by the Yacht Clubs. I'm out."

"What do you mean?" asked Abrahams.

"To catch him," said Hank.

CHAPTER II

THE PROPOSITION

HE sat down and lit a cigarette. The others showed little surprise or interest, with the exception of George du Cane.

It seemed to George that this was a new kind of proposition coming in these dull times.

"Are you in earnest?" said he.

"I sure am," said Hank.

Abrahams, who was over forty with an expanding waist-line, and Carolus, who was a creature dead when divorced from cities and the atmosphere of Art, laughed.

Hank cocked his eye at them. Then he rose to his feet. "I was joking," said Hank, "believe I could make you ginks swallow anything. Well, I'm off, see you to-morrow."

George du Cane followed him out.

In the street he linked arms with him.

"Where are you going?" asked Hank.

"Wherever you are," said George.

"Well, I'm going to the office," said Hank.

"I'll go with you," said George. "I've got an idea."

"What's your idea?" asked Hank.

"I'll tell you when we get to your office," replied George.

Fisher and Company's offices were situated as near heaven as the ordinary American can hope to reach. An express elevator shot them out on a concrete-floored landing where the faint clacking of typewriters sounded from behind doors marked with the names of business firms. The Bolsover Trust Syndicate; Moss Muriatti and Moscovitch; Fisher and Co.

The Fisher offices consisted of two rooms, the outer room for a typewriter and an inner room for the company.

The company's room contained four chairs and a desk-table, a roll-topped desk and a cuspidor. The bare walls were hung with maps of towns and places. There was a map of San Francisco and its environments reaching from Valego to Santa Clara. There were maps of Redwood and San Jose, Belmont and San Mateo, Oakland and San Rafael and others.

George looked at the maps, whilst Hank sat down and looked at the morning's correspondence spread on the table by the office boy.

These maps and town plans, marked here and there with red ink, spoke of big dealings and a prosperous business; the trail of Fisher and Company was over them all. They interested George vastly. It was the first time he had been in the office.

"I say, old man," said George, suddenly breaking silence and detaching himself from the maps. "I didn't know you had a company attached to you. Where's the company?"

"Well, I expect it's in Europe by this," said Hank, laying down the last of his letters. "Or sunning itself on Palm Beach, or listening to the band somewhere. It bolted with the cash box three weeks ago, leaving me a thousand dollars to carry on with."

"Good Lord," said George, horror-stricken, yet amazed at the coolness of the other and the way he had managed to keep his disaster concealed from all and sundry; for at the Club Hank was considered a man of substance, almost too much substance for a Bohemian.

"It's true," said Hank.

"How many men were in it?"

"No men, it was a woman."

"You were in partnership with a woman?"

"Yep."

"Well, she might have done worse," said George, "she might have married you."

Hank, by way of reply, took a photograph from a drawer in the table and handed it to George, who gazed at it for half a minute and handed it back.

"I see," said he, "but what made you have anything to do with her?"

The town lot speculator tilted back in his chair and lit a cigarette.

"Driscoll was her name," said he, "and she didn't care about her looks, she used to boast she could put a whole potato in her mouth. She was my landlady when I lived in Polk Street and she ran a laundry and had a hand in ward politics and the whole of the Irish contingent at her back. She had a better business head on her than any man in 'Frisco, and when I made some money over that trap of mine, she started me in the real estate business. We were good partners and made big money—and now she's bolted."

"Have you set the police after her?"

"Gosh, no," said Hank. "What do you take me for? She's a woman."

"But she's boned your money."

"Half of it was hers, and anyhow, she's a woman. I'm not used to kicking women and I don't propose to learn."

George remembered what Carolus had said about the Female Sanctity business and did not pursue the subject.

Hank smoked, his chair tilted back, his heels on the desk. Ruin seemed to sit easy on the town lot speculator. His mind seemed a thousand miles away from San Francisco and worry.

Then George broke into his reverie. "Look here," he said, "I told you in the street I had an idea. Are you going after this man Vanderdecken or not?"

"And what if I am?" asked the cautious Hank.

"Then I'll join you, if you'll let me."

"Well," said Hank, "I told those two ginks at the Club I wasn't. They've no understanding, for one thing, and for another I don't want them to be spreading the news. But I am. For one thing I want a holiday and for another I want that twenty-five thousand dollars. Twenty, I mean, for it will take me all of five thousand dollars to catch him."

"How much have you?"

"One thousand, about, and then I've got my royalties for the trap coming in."

"That rat trap thing?"

"Yep."

"How much does it bring you a year, if it's not rude to ask?"

"Well, I reckon to net in royalties about one thousand five hundred a quarter and the returns are rising. The British are taking to it and Seligmann's had an order for five thousand traps only last week for London delivery. I can borrow from them in advance of royalties."

George sat down on a chair and nursed his knee and contemplated the toe of his boot. George, despite his easy way of life was no fool in money matters.

"You are going to spend five thousand in trying to catch this pirate," said he, "and if you fail, where will you be?"

"Ask me another," said Hank.

George took his cigarette case from his pocket, chose a cigarette and lit it; the two sat for a moment in silence.

"Besides," said George suddenly, "you'll most likely get a bullet through your head."

"Most like," said Hank.

"To say nothing of weather. You know what Pacific weather is on the coast here, and you'll have to lay up maybe months waiting for the fellow in a cramped boat with beastly grub."

"Sure," said Hank.

"Well, there it is, the whole thing's mad, rotten mad, it hasn't a sound plank in it. What did you mean dragging me here with that proposition for bait?"

"Me drag you!" cried the outraged Hank.

"Yes, you, doped me and dragged me here with your talk at the Club, turned my head till I'm sure not sane, for I'm in this business with you up to the neck. I'm as mad as yourself, I want to be off, I wouldn't be out of it for ten thousand dollars, though I'm hanged if I know what the draw is."

"Man hunting," said Hank.

CHAPTER III

THE PLAN

THE town lot speculator took his feet down from the desk and George, flinging his cigarette away, got up, took a few paces, and altered his position by straddling his chair, leaning his arms on the back. It was a favourite trick of old Harley du Cane. When big things were on, and if there was a crisis and he was seated and talking to you, ten to one he'd get up, take a few paces, and then sit down again straddling his chair as if he were riding a horse.

"Well, that's settled," said George. "I'm with you. What's your plan? You said you knew where this man is and could put your finger on him."

"I guess I was talking through my hat," said Hank. "It's a way I have, times."

"Then how the devil are you going to find him?"

"It's a way I have, times," said Hank, not seeming to hear the other, "but I'm never far wrong when I'm talking that way. I don't know where the chap is any more than I know where Solomon's aunt's buried, but I've a feeling that his haunt's round about the islands down Santa Catalina way. I know all the coast running from Monterey right to Cape St. Lucas. I had a tenth share in a shark boat once, and I've nosed into all the cricks and corners right to the end of Lower California, and I've got a feeling that the Dutchman's using the Channel Islands and that we'll fetch him somewhere about there, if we're clever."

"You're sure it's Amsterdam Joe we're after?"

"No, I'm not."

"But great Scott, you *said* you were sure."

"I was talking," said Hank, "the words were hit out of me by something outside my head, but I'm never far wrong when I'm taken like that. I'd bet a thousand to a nickel it's him, but that's not being sure. You see, it's not Dutch Pete, for I saw him shot with my own eyes, but the affair was hushed up, and they gave his name different in the papers. He was hand and fist with Joe and that's what put the wrong idea about. Joe went south more than nine months ago, superintending a fishery or something down there, and he hasn't come back, and he's just the chap to fill this bill—and there you are."

"Well, it doesn't much matter," said George, "as long as a man's there and will put up a fight and we have the fun of catching him. Now then, Hank F., what are your plans? Spit them out."

"Well," said Hank, "my plans are simple enough. I'm going to drop down to the Islands and do some fishing and water-lily around picking up information where I can. There's all sorts of boats down south of the Islands, doing shark fishing and going after the sulphur-bottom whales; and at Avalon and San Clemente and places there's lots of fellows I can pick up information from. A police boat or a destroyer would find nothing but shut heads, but a man that knows how to go about it can tap the wires. Why, you wouldn't believe how news goes about along the coast, and the long-shoremen are pirates by instinct. There's not one of them isn't backing old man Vanderdecken. Pirates by instinct, only they haven't the pluck of their opinions.

"Well, when I've got this bird's fishing waters, I'm going to lay in them and cruise round in them and whistle 'Chase me Charlie' till he pounces, or maybe I'll be able to put my finger on the creek or bay or wherever it is he makes his port of call, and pounce myself—no knowing."

"I see," said George.

"I'm blessed if I do," said Hank. "It's mighty problematical, but I've got the feeling in my toes that I'm going to collar him."

"Well," said George, "we've got so far. Now about the boat."

"What boat?"

"Well, you don't propose to swim after the Dutchman, do you?"

"Well," said Hank, "if one cog goes wrong in this business, we may both be swimming after him, begging to be took aboard and him using us for target practice—but I'm not going in a boat."

"Then what the devil are you going in?"

"A yacht. Y. A. C. H. T. Sixty ton schooner, auxiliary engine, white-painted boat, turning a bit cream with wear, cabin upholstered in red plush, bird's-eye maple panels let in with pictures of flowers—everything up-to-date, seemingly. She jumped into my head at the Club as I was talking about old Vanderdecken, that's how things come to me. No sooner had I left the 'phone and began talking to you fellows than the whole of this expedition and how to do it hit me on the head like an orange."

"Well, let's get back to business. You have your eye on a yacht, but, from your specification, fifty thousand dollars is more like what you'll want than five. What's the name of this yacht?"

"She's not exactly a yacht," said Hank.

"Then what is she?"

"She's more in the nature of an optical delusion."

George had patience. He had also plenty of time and could afford to let Hank play about. It was the first time he had come really in touch with the town lot speculator's mentality, and it interested him. His own position began to interest him, too. He had pledged himself to this expedition and he would no more draw out than old Harley du Cane would have drawn out of one of his frontal attacks on Jay Gould, however dangerous.

"Well, you are going to chase after this Dutchman in an optical delusion," said he. "I'm listening—go on, spit out your meaning."

Hank rose to his feet and took his hat.

"Come on," said he, "and I'll show you it."

CHAPTER IV

TYREBUCK

THEY left the building and struck down Market Street. It was three o'clock in the afternoon and a blazing day. Market Street looked the same as ever—with a difference. It seemed to George that the whole world had somehow a different tinge, as though he were looking at it from the windows of a lunatic asylum.

The people in the street all seemed to be bent on business, serious and sane beyond ordinary; even the loafers and pleasure-seekers were bathed in this atmosphere.

Said Hank, as they crossed the street towards a block of buildings topped by a huge sky sign advising people to smoke Duke Orlando cigarettes:

"Did you ever read about the one horse shay?"

"Which?" asked George.

"The one that went a hundred years and then bust up."

"No."

"Well, it was made of such good stuff that it couldn't break down, not one part before another, so when the time came it busted up all together."

"What's that got to do with our business?"

"Oh, I was just thinking," said Hank.

They were in the building now. Hank gave a name to the elevator man, and they were whisked up to the fourth floor. Here, entering an office filled with the clatter of typewriters, Hank asked for Mr. Tyrebuck, and in a minute or two they were shown into a room where a man sat facing them at a desk table, a heavy-jowled, bulging-eyed, fresh-coloured man, with an unlighted cigar between his lips. He had just finished with a stenographer, but she was still standing waiting with a sheaf of notes in her hand, whilst Tyrebuck, as if engaged with some after-thought, sat, the cigar pushing out on his under lip and his prominent eyes staring straight at the newcomers without seeing them. He seemed to be looking at something a thousand miles away. He was. He was looking at Chicago and the dial of the Wheat Pit. Then he came to.

"That will do," said he to the stenographer. "Well, Hank, how's the world using you?"

George was introduced, cigars were handed round and they talked. George did the listening. Tyrebuck owned steamers and mines and was engaged just then on a wheat deal. He was one of the busiest men on the Pacific coast and one of the wealthiest, but he found time to talk to Hank. Tyrebuck talked as if he had absolutely nothing to do. They talked of the weather and President Wilson and Europe. Hank, who had been in England during the war, outlined a plan of his for taking over the British Empire, electrifying it, steam-heating it, fitting it with elevators, speaking tubes and American business methods. Then he rose. "Well, I must be going," said Hank. "But say, what I came about was the *Wear Jack*. I saw her only day before yesterday down at Sullivan's Wharf."

"Oh, did you?" said Tyrebuck, "blessed if I hadn't clean forgot her. Is she hanging together?"

"Well, she was, the day before yesterday. I'm open to hire her."

"What's your idea—put her on wheels?"

"Nope. I've got an expedition on down south. You've heard of this man Vanderdecken?"

"Sure."

"Well, I'm going down to catch him."

"Humph," said Tyrebuck, "you'll go down right enough in the *Wear Jack* if the putty gives."

"That's what I was telling Mr. du Cane," said Hank. "She's not so much a yacht as an optical delusion. She looks A 1, but isn't, but we're going to take a whale boat."

"Why not go in the whale boat?" asked Tyrebuck. "What you want taking the *Wear Jack* along—for fun?"

"It's part of my plan to have a yacht," replied the other, "and she looks like a yacht—Oh, she's not so bad—it was only my joke. I reckon she'll hold together as long as we want her, the sticks look sound enough."

"Well, she mayn't be as bad as she's painted," agreed Tyrebuck. "I've been too busy to bother with her. I bought her as old junk, thinking to pull off a deal, and had her fixed up by Michelson and advertised her. Her lines are lovely, there's no denying that. You remember last fall I took you down with Cookson to look at her and he went about prodding her with a knife. He offered four thousand for her."

"Oh, he did, did he?" said Hank.

"Well, he was secretary of the Brookland Creek Yacht Club and they wanted her for a floating annex. When I refused, he got impudent and said the members wouldn't have anything to do with the deal as they weren't a suicide club. That joke got about."

"I heard it," said Hank.

"It crabbed her. All the smarties got busy guying her and me, and I got a letter from a chap calling himself Charon and offering ten dollars for her as a house boat on the Styx, and so it went on till everybody forgot her, but it has dished any chance of a deal. Mention her to any yachtsman and all those damned old jokes flutter up like moths; it's like a woman's reputation. Once it's damaged, there's no use in shaking it out of the window and putting new buttons on it—there's no buyers."

Hank agreed. "Well, what's your terms?" said he at last.

"Ten thousand dollars," said Tyrebuck.

"Is she insured?"

"She's insured for ten thousand dollars. I pushed her through with the insurance agents that do my steamboat work."

"But I don't want to buy her. I want to charter her."

"Well, I can't charter boats, not even to you, Hank, it's against my principles. Why, if I were to charter the old *Wear Jack* and the fact got round, I'd be guyed out of 'Frisco. Can't you hear them at the Club asking me how the long-shore business was doing and what price the hire of canoes. No, sir, I've had enough of the joke business over that damned sieve. There she sticks till I sell her and the price is ten thousand, not a cent under."

George du Cane felt the lifting of a weight from his mind. The deal was evidently off. He had only to put his hand in his pocket, so to say, and fetch out the ten thousand, but the idea of a cruise in the *Wear Jack* had begun to fill his mind with frank and honest alarm. Besides, he knew that Hank would accept no outside financial help or interference. This was his show, to be engineered and run by himself. Feeling safe, he indulged in a little show off.

"That's a pity," said he, "I shouldn't have minded risking it; besides, we'd have had the whale boat, but I suppose it can't be helped."

He spoke without knowledge of the intricacy and subtlety of the rat trap inventor's mental works.

"I've got it," said Hank, "you can loan her to me."

Tyrebuck, who seemed suddenly to remember that he had been smoking an unlighted cigar all this time, was in the act of striking a match. He lit the cigar, blew a cloud of smoke and placed the dead match carefully on a tray by the Billikin on his desk. Then he said:

"Well I'm damned, Hank, if you don't take the cake. You do indeed, you do indeed, you take the cake with the cherry topknot. You come here to me in the temple, so to say, of business propositions—"

"That's what I'm bringing you," said Hank. "A business proposition on the hook, warranted sound, free from scab—it's a buffalo."

"Trot out your buffalo," said Tyrebuck.

"Well, it's this way," said Hank. "You lend me the *Wear Jack*. If she busts up and never comes back, you get your insurance, don't you? If we bring her back with the Dutchman on board, she's a hero and you have the laugh over the whole waterside. Even if we don't collar the Dutchman and come back, she'll have proved herself seaworthy and I'll give her a certificate all round the town that'll sell her for you in two hours."

"Gosh!" groaned Tyrebuck, "why didn't I insure her for twenty thousand?" He wallowed in thought for a moment, then he said:

"Hank."

"Yep?"

"D'you want a partnership in a shipping business?"

"Nope."

"Well, if you do, I'll take you on. I will, sure. Yes, you can have the loan of her. God help the Dutchman if you're after him. Take her down south, take her to blazes, take her anywhere you like and now get out of my office for I'm busy. One moment, here's my card, there's a watchman on board her, show him this and he'll let you go over her and I'll send you a letter to-night confirming the loan."

Outside Hank took George's arm. "Say, Bud, you're the right sort."

"How so?" asked George.

"I don't believe there's another man in 'Frisco that would have gone in with me on this, not on that specification anyhow. D'y' know the *Wear Jack* was built in 'sixty-seven."

"What do you mean by 'sixty-seven?"

"Three years before the first German-French war. It's on the shipwright's plate on the after gratings. 'Duncan Matheson, 1867,' that's her birth certificate. One of the first yacht-building firms to start in 'Frisco."

George said nothing, but he was thinking a lot.

"I had it in my mind that he'd have chartered her," went on Hank, "it's lucky he shied at that idea for I hadn't thought of the whale boat. Why, between the whale boat and provisions and crew, it'll take nearly all that five thousand dollars."

"You wouldn't care to take a *bigger* boat?" said George. "I'll finance the business or go shares."

"Oh, she's big enough," said Hank, "and this is my show. I'm doing it on my own hook; otherwise I'd have no interest in it. I'm awfully lucky to have got you, for you're a millionaire, aren't you, Bud, and you won't want a hand in the profits, besides being the only man in 'Frisco that'd take the risks for the fun of the thing."

"I believe I am," said George, unenthusiastically.

CHAPTER V

JAKE

THE water front of San Francisco is unique. The long wharves, vibrating to the thunder of trade, show ships from all corners of the world; ships from China and the Islands, from Japan, from Africa, from India; tall Cape Horners, held to the wharves with wire mooring-lines, lie cleaning their bilges or lining their holds for grain cargoes with ships for Durban, ships for Cork, steamers for Seattle and Northern ports. Beyond lies the bay, blue or wind-beaten gray, busy with a shipping life of its own, with Oakland, six miles across the water, for a sister port. Beyond the bay are the hills that saw the desolation before the first Spaniards broke the ground or the keel of the first sandalwood trader rode the waters of the Golden Gate.

Here on the wharves to-day, it takes little imagination to see the ships that have vanished and the traders that are gone—the South Sea whaleman, with stump top gallant masts and boats slung out on wooden davits, the Island schooner of the old days when the *Leonora* was a living ship and before copra was handled by companies.

George and his companion struck the water front, where a big "turret boat" of the Clan line was moored, the Lascars huddled round her foc'sle engaged in preparing fish for a curry.

"That's the canal," said Hank. "She's come through from 'Urope with a cargo and now she's loading up for Bombay or somewhere. Looks as if she'd been built by some one that'd gone bughouse, don't she? She's built like that to save dues going through the Suez Canal. Wonder what the shipping companies will be up to in the way of swindling the Panama. I tell you, Bud, there's not a hair's difference between humans and rats for tricks and smart ways."

They passed along, reaching an old decayed bit of wharf that had somehow withstood change and reconstruction. It is now little more than a landing stage, but in the old days, under the name of Rafferty's wharf, it had a broad front. Whalers used to come alongside to discharge and clean up and here Bones' Old Sailors' Lodging House, half tavern, used to take unfortunates in and do for them. There was a trap door from Bones' back parlour to the water below, where boats could come in between the piles and ship off sailor men blind with dope. Then it became respectable and changed its name to Sullivan's.

Alongside this stage lay the *Wear Jack*, a sixty ton schooner, fifty feet long. The watchman happened to be on deck, a thin man greatly gone to decay, dressed in a brown sweater and wearing an old fur cap. He was seated on the coaming of the skylight, smoking.

"Hullo," said Hank. "That you, Jake?"

The fellow below cocked an eye up and evidently recognised the other, but he didn't move.

"I'm coming aboard to overhaul her," said Hank. "I've just seen Mr. Tyrebuck, here's his card."

"Well, I'm not preventin' you," said Jake.

Hank came down the ladder followed by George.

The deck of the *Wear Jack* ran flush fore and aft. Neglect sat there with dirt and tobacco juice. Old ends of rope lay about and spars and main blocks that had seen a better day, and bits of newspaper and a bucket with potato peelings in it.

Forward, with her keel to the sky, lay an old broken dinghy that might have come out of the ark, and a flannel jumper aired itself on the port rail. No wonder that prospective buyers sniffed and went off.

The soft job man on the cabin skylight looked at the newcomers.

"Where's your cyard?" said he.

Hank presented the card. "Now then," said Hank, "if you're not stuck to that skylight with cobbler's wax, hoist yourself and get busy. I'm going right all over her, cabin first. Come along."

He led the way down.

The saloon of the *Wear Jack* had plenty of head room, six feet four or so; there were bunks on either side and a cabin aft shut off by a bird's-eye maple door. The upholstering was in crimson, crimson plush, and the table was of mahogany. Everything was of the best and little the worse for wear, but over everything was the gloom of the murdered sunlight, filtering in through the filthy skylight and the grimy portholes. Hank opened the door of the after cabin.

"Pretty musty, ain't it?" said Jake. "I kyan't get it right, nohow. You could grow mushrooms on that bunk with the damp, though where it comes from, search me. Ain't sea damp, it's damp that seems to have got in the wood. The wood sweats when the weather's a bit warm. Smells like an old cheese."

"Well, I ain't buying a scent factory," said Hank.

"Oh, buyin' her, are you?" said Jake, "*buyin'* her." He said nothing more, but followed as Hank led the way out of the saloon. They inspected the lavatory and bath, the galley, and then they came to the auxiliary engine, for the *Wear Jack* boasted an auxiliary engine, a neat little Kelvin paraffin engine in a canvas jacket.

"Does the engine run?" asked Hank of the soft job man.

"Run," said Jake. "Well the last time I heard of it runnin', it run off its bed plates. That's the yarn I got from one of the chaps that were in her on her last cruise—but maybe it's a lie."

"Now look here," said Hank, "you deal straight with me and I'll deal straight with you to the tune of five dollars. I don't want to buy old junk. Is there anything wrong with this ship?" He nudged George as he spoke.

"Well," said Jake, "I oughtn't to be talking, I s'pose, I'm put here to show her to parties, but I haven't swore to say nothing; anything wrong with her? Why she's all wrong, the sticks are carrots and the plankin's mush, run that there injin and you'll shake her to pieces, get her in a beam sea and she'll strain her heart open. But mind you she's fast, her lines are good, but they're just lines held together by a lick of paint."

Hank was down on his knees testing the planking to which the bed plates were fixed with his knife.

Then he rose up and led the way on deck. They examined the foc'sle. It had accommodations for six.

Coming out of the foc'sle, Hank began a cruise of his own, poking about here and there. Then he dived down below again.

When he came on deck he handed Jake the five dollars for his information and they left the ship.

He took George's arm as they went along the wharf.

"Remember," said he, "what I told you to-day about the *Wear Jack* being an optical delusion."

"Yes, and you seem to have been pretty right."

"Oh, was I? Well, way back in my head I was thinking different, and I only know that now. I can't explain my head piece, except by saying it goes by instinct. When I saw Jake the other day, he must have climbed right down into my mind and sat there ever since, explaining things without my knowing, otherwise I'm doubtful if I'd have been so keen on Tyrebuck letting me have the old *Jack*. Not that I mind risking my life, but there it is, I wouldn't have been as keen and maybe wouldn't have pushed the deal through. It's the biggest deal I've ever made."

"How's that?"

"Why, Bud, can't you see what's wrong with the schooner?"

"No."

"Jake! The schooner's as sound as I am. She's not as young as she used to be, but she's one of the old navy that was built to wear. I've examined her. You remember my telling you that rats couldn't beat humans in tricks? Well, it was just beginning to hit me then that maybe all that raffle and dirt on her deck and all the yarns I'd heard about her were put out by Jake."

"Why?"

"Why, to keep his job. He don't want her sold. She's his job. Besides, he's been collecting five dollars a time, and maybe more, from every mug of a buyer he's given 'a straight tip' about her. That's human nature. He wouldn't have got a cent for praising her."

"Good Lord! What a scoundrel! Why didn't you tell him straight out instead of handing him that money?"

"Not me," said Hank. "Have him maybe sink her at her moorings to-night, or play some dirty trick. To-morrow, with Tyrebuck's letter in my hand, it will be different. But only for him, I wouldn't have got her for nothing."

"Only for yourself, you mean," said George.

"Well, maybe," said Hank.

CHAPTER VI

JOE BARRETT

THE DU CANE house on Pacific Avenue was—is, in fact—a monstrous affair, at least viewed as the residence of a single man. Old Harley's tastes were big and florid and he had entertained on a large scale; at his death George would have sold or let the place, but something held him, maybe Harley's ghost, for the old man's personality was so strong that it had imprinted itself everywhere, so that to sell or let the place would, so George felt, have been equivalent almost to selling or letting the old man himself.

George had closed a lot of the rooms, cutting down the servants to four or five in number, reserving for himself only a sitting-room and a bedroom, a dressing-room and bathroom.

This morning, the morning after the Jake business, he was awakened by a knock at the door and the entrance of his valet Farintosh. He had picked up Farintosh in England as a sort of curio. He had been his valet at the Carlton Hotel. Farintosh's father had been own man to the Marquis of Bristol, his grandfather butler to the Duke of Hamilton, his brother was head waiter at Boodle's and his sister in service at Sandringham House. He had small side whiskers.

Farintosh, having closed the door cautiously, announced that a gentleman of the name of Fisher had called to see George and was waiting in the sitting-room.

"What's the time?" asked George.

"Half past seven, sir."

George lay back with a groan.

"Show him right in here," said he.

George, on parting from Hank the day before, had dined with some friends at the Palatial. Released from the hypnotism of the town lot speculator, he had begun to cool ever so slightly over the Vanderdecken business. The cooling had gone on during sleep. Awakened, an hour before his usual time, to the ordinary facts of life, his feet were frankly cold. Shultz, the man he had dined with at the Palatial, was going off to the Rockies on a shooting expedition and had asked him to join. There would be plenty of fun and plenty of sport—yet he had to refuse.

But there was something more than that, Farintosh. The absolutely sane and correct Farintosh acted as an underscore to the whole of this business.

Farintosh, whose lips rarely said more than "Yes, sir," or "No, sir," was voiceful in all sorts of subtle ways, as, for instance, when he had announced a "gentleman of the name of Fisher."

Entered Hank, suddenly, backed by Farintosh, who closed the door on the pair.

"Say, Bud, ain't you up yet?" cried Hank. "Why, I've been running round since five. Say—shall I pull the blinds?" He pulled them up, letting in a blaze of early sunlight. Then he looked round the room, took in its magnificence and seemed to wilt a bit. He sat down on a chair.

"Who's the old boy with the whiskers?" he asked.

George explained, yawning, and Hank, without waiting to hear him out, went on. He seemed suddenly to have recovered his confidence in himself; the radium-like activity of his mind broke forth, and he talked the other out of bed, into the bathroom and through his bathing and shaving operations. If you had been listening, you would have heard George's contributions to the conversation, at first monosyllabic, then in words of more than one syllable, then in long sentences. He was losing his cold feet, blossoming again in the atmosphere of Hank, for Hank was at once an individual and an atmosphere, an atmosphere wherein extraordinary ideas, seeming scarcely strange, could flourish like tropical plants in a green house.

At breakfast, George was his same old self again and as keen as yesterday about the Dutchman business.

"I didn't tell you," said the Rat Trap Inventor, "I've been cooking it up—but I've done another deal. Y'remember I said I'd want five thousand dollars to push the thing through? Well, now listen, you saw what I did with Tyrebuck, well I've done better with Barrett."

"Which Barrett?"

"Joe."

Instantly before George's eyes arose the picture of Barrett's Stores on Market Street in all their vastness, and Joe Barrett himself, dapper and debonair. Eccentric by nature, Barrett used his eccentricity as a means toward publicity. If he had possessed a wooden leg or a glass eye or a skeleton in his cupboard, he would without doubt have used them as a means of advertisement. It was the only thing he really cared for. His business was less to him than the advertising of it; heaven for J. B. existed only as a background for sky signs and if he could have printed "Barrett" on the moon in indelible ink, he would have done so, even at the risk of being skinned alive by all the poets.

"Yes?" said George.

"I met him last night at the Bay Club," said Hank, "and the idea struck me. He'd provision us better and cheaper than anyone else seeing that I know him so well. He's a sport, and I just let him into the thing, told him the whole business and how I'd got the *Wear Jack* from Tyrebuck for nothing and how you were joining in. Then I opened my batteries about the provisions. I want enough for six men for three months, to say nothing of gasoline and oil and some new bunk bedding. He offered to do it for two thousand dollars. I offered a thousand, to take him down, and he forked out a dollar. 'I'll toss you two thousand or nothing,' he says. Luck seemed running so strong I took him, and lost."

"Oh, you lost."

"One minute. 'Best out of three,' said he, and tosses again. I won; then he tosses again and I won. You see he'd got it in his head, somehow, that we were tossing best out of three, either that or he wanted me to win. I tell you, he's a sport. The Dutchman proposition had taken such a hold on him I guess he wanted to help, somehow. Anyhow, there it is; boat and provisions won't cost me a cent. How's that for luck?"

"Good," said George laughing. "And now if you get a crew for nothing, you'll be fixed."

"Well, I've got you for one," said Hank. "You won't cost anything and you can steer."

George put down his coffee cup.

"That reminds me," said he, "how about the navigation—are you any good?"

"Well, I don't say I'm good," said Hank, "but I'm good enough to take that old cat boat down the coast and bring her back again. Now if you're finished, let's get, for I'm just longing to begin the sweep of her decks and start clearing her down and overhauling the rigging."

"But see here," said George, "aren't you going to get men to work on her?"

"Yep. I'm a man, aren't I, and you're another. Now, you get it in your head, Bud: I'm starting out in this business to catch the Dutchman, not to support a lot of bone lazy union fumblers for half their natural. Why you don't know what these dockyard dandies are, you don't indeed. Y' remember Elihu Stevens when he started out on that cruise of his in the *Maryland*? I've seen him near crying over the dollar-snatchers at work on her. They robbed him of time and they robbed him of money, and they damn near robbed him of his life with their rotten spars and mush planking."

"But I'm as innocent as Solomon's aunt of how rigging should be fixed."

"I'll learn you," said Hank.

George was silent. He seemed thinking about things. Hank leaned forward across the table.

"Bud," said he, "you're not backing out, are you? You're not afraid of a bit of work? Why, look here, Bud, I'd only to put my hand in your pocket, so to speak, and pull out the dollars to pay for fitters and riggers enough to fit out a battleship, let alone the *Wear Jack*. But, leaving alone being robbed of time and dollars, where'd be the game in that? I'm doing this thing with my own hands and head and so are you. Forget money—it spoils everything."

"You're pretty keen after it all the same, Hank," said George laughing.

"Yep. When I'm chasing it, but I'm not chasing it now, I'm chasing the Dutchman. I'm not thinking of the twenty-five thousand, I'm thinking of the Dutchman. It's a game and I don't want money to help me. Why, I'd blush to be helped by money in chasing a man, unless he'd done me some wrong. When I get this fellow by the scruff, I wanta say to myself, 'Hank, you took this man by the work of your own hands and your own head, and against odds. He had as good chances as you, and you didn't shoot him sitting.' If you don't take me, Bud, then we don't understand each other and I'll leave you to that gink with the whiskers and your millionaire ways and start off on my lonesome."

"We understand each other," said George, ringing the bell. "I'm not afraid of a bit of work with my hands. Farintosh."

"Yes, sir."

"Send round the car."

In the hall, as they passed out to the car, Hank picked up a bundle he had brought with him.

"What's in that?" asked George.

"Overalls," said Hank.

They drew up in Malcolm Street close to the wharves.

"Take her back," said George to the chauffeur, "and tell Farintosh to come along at half-past twelve with enough sandwiches for two and a bottle of—Oh, damn—two bottles of lemonade. You can drink lemonade, Hank?"

"Sure."

"Tell him he'll find me in the yacht that's moored at Sullivan's wharf. It's close to this place, he can't mistake."

The car drove off, and they started for the water side, Hank carrying the bundle.

CHAPTER VII

THE FIRING OF JAKE

THE street was blazing with the morning light, and, turning a corner, a puff of wind from the bay hit George in the face. It carried with it a scent of tar, oakum and bilge, and it was like the breath of the great god Adventure himself, the god of morning and unknown places and strange happenings.

It felt good to be alive, and the clearing up of a ratty old yacht with Hank Fisher, seemed the joyfullest business on earth. Hank had hit a big nail on the head. Money would have spoiled this show—just as it spoils most shows.

They passed along the wharf till they reached Sullivan's. Hank dumped his bundle and came to the side and George, following him, saw Jake.

Jake was fishing.

"Hullo," said Hank.

"Hullo," said Jake.

"Caught anything?" said Hank.

"Naw—fish ain't bitin'."

"Well, I'm sorry for that, for I've taken over the fishing rights. Jake, you're fired, the yacht's mine, I've taken her over and you've got to get."

"Y' mean to say you've bought her?"

"Nope. Mr. Tyrebuck has loaned her to me. It's all the same, you've got to get. Here's his letter, want to read it?"

He dropped the typewritten letter down and Jake spelled over it. Then he said: "And how about the pay due to me, you goin' to settle?"

"Nope—McCallum's will pay you. Better go to them, they'll be glad to see you for I told them what you said about her."

"And what did I say about her?"

"Told me her spars were carrots and her planking mush."

"That's a damned lie," said Jake, "and if there's law to be had in 'Frisco, I'll have you for it, b'gob."

"Told me she'd open out first beam sea—now then, you dog-eyed squateroo, get your dunnage and clear, pronto."

George had never seen Hank heated until this. His eyes blazed and his lean face filled with venom as he looked down on the man who had tried to crab the *Wear Jack*.

Jake tried to meet his gaze, failed, collected his dunnage, drew in his fishing line and scrambled ashore.

"If there's law to be had in 'Frisco, I'll have you for this," cried he.

Hank dropped the bundle of overalls on to the deck and they followed it.

"Swab," said Hank.

Then they put on the overalls. Hank started his cleaning up with an axe. There was an axe lying in the starboard scuppers, and, seizing it, he made for the old dinghy.

"Go hunt for a mop," he cried to the other. "I saw one down below. Can't dump this old bath tub into the harbour as she is or there'll be trouble. B'sides I want exercise."

He began to set the rotten planks flying with the axe, whilst George fetched the mop, also a bucket, which, under the direction of the perspiring Hank, he fastened to a rope so that they could dip up water for deck swilling. The remains of the dinghy overboard, they turned to on the raffle; rope ends, dead and done blocks, old newspapers, bits of coal.

"Why, look you here," said Hank, holding up one of the blocks, "look at the size of it. It must have belonged to a three-master as old as the ark. That guy's been hunting the wharves for old raffle to dump aboard her and make a litter; stick it in the sail room for evidence if he starts any law bother. Now, gimme that bucket."

The swilling and swabbing of the deck began and continued till the dowels showed up in the planking. Then they rested and smoked cigarettes. It was now noon, and George, as he sat on the coaming of the cabin skylight, resting and watching the planking dry in the sun, felt uplifted. Since leaving the army he hadn't done a hand's turn of honest work, simply because he could not find any work to do. There are a surprising number of rich people out of work owing to no fault of their own, unemployed men and women with big bank balances starving for employment. The war was a simple Godsend to these. It supplied them with a reason and an initiative. Hank had supplied George with both these things.

Then, now that the decks were cleared up, the *Wear Jack* began to speak to him as only a ship can speak to a man. She was no longer a dirty hulk but a live thing awakening from sleep, a thing with the mobility of a bird, a sister of the sea and the wind. He had been on many a yacht and many a steamboat as guest or passenger, but this was the first ship he had ever got close to. The work with the mop and bucket, the knowledge that he would soon be helping to rig her and handle her, the sight of her now that she was cleaning up, the very smell of her, all combined to work the charm. He went below to heave the old block into the sail room and when he came on deck again Hank was up like a cat in the rigging, hunting for rotten ratlines, a knife between his teeth.

At one o'clock Farintosh appeared with the sandwiches; at five o'clock they knocked off. They had cleared and cleaned the deck, made an overhaul of the rigging, cleared and cleaned the cabin, and cleaned the bathroom and lavatory.

"I'll start on the rigging to-morrow," said Hank. "It's all sound but a few ropes and ratlines—Christopher!"

"What?"

"I've fired the watchman and who's to look after her?"

"Oh, she won't hurt."

"Won't hurt! Why, if you fell asleep on these wharves, they'd have your back teeth before you woke and you wouldn't feel them pulling them. Why, these hooligans, if they didn't strip her, they'd camp in her, and then she'd be no more mortal use till she was boiled. No. I guess I'll have to stick to her."

"Stick to her!" cried George, "you mean to say, sleep here?"

"Yep. What's wrong? The old bunk bedding will do me and the nights are warm. To-morrow I'll get a man to look after her for a few hours in the evening whilst I get my dunnage aboard. Come along ashore with me while I get some grub and a toothbrush."

He slipped out of his overalls and they climbed ashore.

"She won't take any harm for an hour or two by herself," said Hank.

They found a street of shops boasting a drug store. Here Hank bought his toothbrush, then he bought a German sausage, some bread, six small apples and two bottles of tonic water, also an evening paper from a yelling newsboy. Then he remembered that he would want a candle to read the newspaper by and went into a ships chandler's to buy one, leaving George outside.

George glanced at the paper, then he spread it open hurriedly and stood reading it, heedless of the passersby or the people who jostled him. Hank, coming out of the store with his candle, looked over George's shoulder and this is what he read, in scare headlines across a double column of print:

HANK FISHER OF THE BOHEMIAN CLUB GOES AFTER THE DUTCHMAN

Joe Barrett Loses on the Deal But Comes Up Smiling at Josh Tyrebuck and Bud du Cane

Then came the details. The dollar tossed at the Bay Club, which gave Hank two thousand dollars' worth of goods for nothing, the loan of the *Wear Jack* by Tyrebuck and George du Cane's participation in the business.

George felt as though all his clothes had suddenly been stripped off him there in the street. Hank whistled.

Then he said: "That's Barrett. Lord, I might have known. He didn't toss fair, he wanted me to win, and now, look! He's got the goods, five thousand dollars' worth of advertising for a thousand dollars' worth of bully beef and canned t'matoes. It won't cost him more than that, for he's giving me the stuff at retail prices. And now it will be all over the town and all over the waterside."

"Curse him," said George. His lips were dry. There was a jocular tone in that confounded press notice that cast a blight on everyone concerned except Joe Barrett. Joe, though he was the only loser of money in the business up to the present was, in some extraordinary way, put on a pedestal as a sport, whilst the others ran round the plinth like figures of fun.

"It's him and his publicity man, Josh Scudder, who've done it," said Hank. "I can tell Josh's hand in it—it's his style. Well, there it is, it can't be helped. I'd planned to slip out quiet and come back with a brass band playing Dutchland under alles and Vanderdecken in leg irons; now the blanket's stripped off us clean. We'll be laughed at from Hell to Hoboken if we don't make good. We're on the toboggan full speed, no use grabbing at the snow. There's only one way out—we've gotta get the Dutchman."

CHAPTER VIII

PUBLICITY

GEORGE did not go to the club that night. He went straight home and sent Farintosh out to buy all the evening papers and Farintosh returned with a bundle of everything from the *Evening Sun* to the *Polk Street Pikers' Messenger*. Every paper had the news, under all sorts of scare headlines. Some of these headlines referred to Fisher and some to himself; through all the notices ran a gentle and breezy humour, and in them all, with one exception, Joe Barrett had his advertisement and walked protected from laughter as Shadrac from flame.

The one exception was the *Polk Street Piker*, a free spoken organ that generally kept to ward politics. The *Piker*, whilst allowing that Rat Trap Fisher had swelled head and had better stick to rodents, was frankly libellous about Barrett, said the whole thing was a fake got up by Barrett to help his sale of damaged goods then on, said a business must be pretty rocky to adopt such means, said that it was likely the whole Dutchman business was a business fake.

George read this horrible libel with a chill at his heart, for he knew that Hennessy, the editor of the *Piker*, was a led captain and creature of Barrett's. No one of any account read the *Piker*, but everyone of any account would read the abject apology of the *Piker* sure to be published in a day or two in every newspaper in California, together with editorial comments and a full statement about the Fisher Expedition supplied by Scudder. The thing would probably reach New York and London. With Vanderdecken as engine and Barrett as driver and stoker, there was no knowing where it might not reach or how long it might not keep running, and he, George du Cane, was tied to the tail of it. He was already in the blaze of the limelight and at that moment men in the clubs, people at dinner parties, people in restaurants and people in cars were talking of him. The fact of his wealth would give him a little place, all his own, in this show. There was only one way of escape—justification. "We've gotta get the Dutchman." Hank's words came back to him. If they did not get the Dutchman, it would be much better not to come back to San Francisco. George had a fine feeling for Pacific Coast temperament; leaving that alone, half frozen Icelanders would see the point and the joke of a much advertised amateur expedition such as theirs returning empty handed.

He went to bed early but he could not sleep for a long time. It was all very well talking about getting the Dutchman, but how were they to get him?

When the getting of him had been only a matter of sport, the thing seemed fairly easy; now that it was a matter of dire necessity, it seemed next to impossible. A nightmare task like hunting for a lost needle in Kearney Street.

He jumped out of bed, fetched an atlas, and, taking it back to bed with him, looked up the California coast, running his eye along from San Francisco to Cape San Lucas, exploring the sea from the Channel Islands to Guadaloupe and from Guadaloupe to the Tres Marias Islands. Somewhere in that vast stretch of sea, somewhere on that line of coast that ran from the Golden Gate to Cancer, they had to find a man who most certainly did not want to be found by searchers. He went to sleep on the thought and awoke to it.

Farintosh was entering the room; he was carrying a bundle of morning papers.

"Pull up the blind," said George.

Propped on the pillows, he opened the first paper to hand expecting to see his name in double leaded type. Not a word. In all the paper not a word of him or Hank or the Dutchman or the expedition. The next paper was the same and the next. The great San Francisco dailies and the little San Francisco dailies had treated the matter with the most absolute contempt. George felt curiously flat, he even looked at the dates of the papers to make sure there was no mistake and that Farintosh had not by some accident brought him yesterday's press.

He had dreaded seeing his name and now he was disappointed because it was not there. Human nature is a funny thing.

He rose, bathed, dressed and came down to breakfast, but still the depression clung. He felt small and of little account, he felt weak and irritable. What was wrong with him? He had tasted Publicity, that is all. Publicity, the wine of the Barretts, is also the wine of the poets; its fascination is universal and of whatever brand it is, from abusive to laudatory, it is always Publicity. Even the pillory, I expect, had its compensations in the old days, and to be recognized with a bad egg or a dead cat was, at all events, to be recognised.

And what a blaze-up that was last night, with every paper screaming round the bon-fire,—and now this frost—why, that alone was in the nature of an insult.

Suddenly and in the act of pouring himself out a second cup of coffee, his mind cleared and his energy returned. "We've gotta get the Dutchman." Hank's words had come back to him. "And by God we will," said he.

He finished his breakfast, rang for the car and started for the wharves. The deck of the *Wear Jack* was empty, he dropped down to the cabin and there was Hank surrounded with newspapers. Hank had evidently purchased largely last night as well as this morning.

"Well," said George lightly, "there's not a word in the morning papers and that's a good thing."

Hank grunted.

"That's Barrett," said he. "He's cut the news off plunk. Why, a blaze in the morning papers would have been out by to-night; as it is every man from Pacific Avenue to Polk Street is saying, 'Why, there ain't no news about Hank.' Barrett's being 'phoned to death at the present minute asking what it all means. People will be talking all day, wanting news of the business and inventing lies to fill the gaps, till it'll get about that the Dutchman's been caught by Joe Barrett an's being exhibited at his stores. By to-night all the 'phones will be humming with lies and all the South Coast papers shouting for information. Why, Bud, where were you born not to know that advertising isn't printing stuff in the papers but making men talk. One big rumour, if you set it going, bumbling away like thunder in the foot hills, is worth all the printed stuff from here to Nome. We're fair handicapped. If I was advertising liver pills, I'd be joyful, but I'm not."

"Think it will queer our pitch?"

"Well, you don't go duck-shooting with a brass band, do you? But there's no use in talking, we're on the slide and we'll have to slither, and brass band or no, I'm going to get him. Come on, we've gotta get to work."

He had been at work since six o'clock, it seemed, on the ratlines, and he was now overhauling all the standing rigging. That done, they attacked the running.

In the middle of these operations it began to dawn on them that they were observed. Sometimes there was quite a little group on the wharf watching and criticising. George noticed it first.

"How the devil have they got to know the whereabouts of the boat?" asked George. "The papers said nothing about Sullivan's Wharf."

"It's Jake," said Hank. "He'll have been all over the wharves talking; take a pull on that halyard. Lord, these blocks will never do, I'll have to go hunt in the sail-room to see if I can't turn out some better. What's the time? Getting on for one? Well, I've got some grub down below and I vote we have a bite, and after that, if you don't mind, will you skip ashore to the club and see if there's any letters for me. I'm expecting a business letter from N' York about a patent I've got an interest in."

"Right," said George.

The galley of the *Wear Jack* was well fitted up. Jake had done his cooking there and had left half a can of kerosene behind him. Hank had got eggs and a great chunk of bacon from somewhere out of the blue, and there was the remains of last night's German sausage. In a few minutes the frying pan was shouting over a Primus stove and Hank, in his shirt sleeves, was directing George. There was a let-down table in the galley and plates and knives and forks in a locker.

"I've overhauled the crockery and table and bed linen," said Hank. "Did it last night. There's enough on board for a family—pass me your plate. We'll have a Chink for cook."

"How about the crew?"

"Time enough about them—maybe we'll have Chinks."

To George, pondering as he ate, suddenly came the fact that Vanderdecken—the Dutchman—Dutch Pete, or whatever his name might be, certainly had behind him a crew of the same colour as himself, coupled with the fact that a crew of Chinks wouldn't be of the same fighting colour as Vanderdecken's lot.

He said so.

"Oh, it won't come to fighting," said Hank. "If it did I can hit a dollar with an automatic at twenty-five paces once a second, and I'll learn you to do the same—but it won't. We've got to take that chap with our wits, not with guns, though they'll be useful maybe for bluff. Did y' ever see strategy and tactics combined in the concrete?"

"No," said George.

"Then you've never seen my rat trap," said Hank.

An hour later George returned from his visit to the club with two letters for Hank. One was the expected letter from New York; the other, which bore only the San Francisco post-mark, was addressed to R. T. Fisher, and ran:

11 West Lincoln Street,
San Francisco.

Sir,
As a lover of the sea and all that therein is, I take this opportunity to beg leave to apply for a post in your expidition, can turn my hand to anything that isn't crooked. Was gold-mining at Klondike two years but give it up owing to a frost bight but am used to dealing with rough characters. Seeing the piece about you in the evening paper to-night I make haist to apply and

you will find me equal prompt in my dealings I have to do with you, and satisfactory. A line to above will oblige.

Yours, truly,
J. B. Yonkers.

P. S. Terms can be arranged.

"That's the bill-mackerel," said Hank. "Did you ever see a mackerel? Well, it's always headed by a couple or so of freak mackerel. Chaps with bills like ducks. This is the first of the shoal of chaps that'll be wanting to come along, with us—you'll see."

CHAPTER IX

CANDON

GEORGE did.

An abject and crawling apology from the *Piker*, published and paid for in next morning's papers, restarted the publicity campaign, and, though the press never recovered its first careless rapture, the thing had made good and was established in the mind of the public. The letters came in day by day, some addressed to the club, some care of Joe Barrett, all of the same tenor. The expedition that had aroused mild merriment in the upper circles of San Francisco was received in dead seriousness by the middle and lower circles— even with enthusiasm. The thing had vast appeal to the movie-red mind; the exploits of the Dutchman, inconsiderable enough in a world where criminal license had suddenly added cubits to its stature, had been boomed by the press. Hank Fisher had already a name to embroider on and "Bud" du Cane was not unknown. Letters came from all round the Bay; from Oakland, Berkeley, Port Costa, New York, California, Antioch, Benicia, San Rafael and Tiburon; letters came from Monterey and all down the coast. Letters from "all sorts and sexes" to put it in Hank's words. Women offered to come along as cooks, boys as "deck-hands," a retired banker at San Jo offered to pay to be taken along. Never in any letter except that of the "bill-mackerel" was there a reference to terms, all these people were ready to go for nothing but their "grub and bunk" as one gentleman put it, and, if you wish to gauge the utility of a personality like Hank's, this vast and healthy wave of adventure-craving which he had set going amongst the populace of the state is an index.

"And not one of the lot is any use," said Hank, as he sat in the cabin with George one day about a week before the projected start. "I saw those people I wrote to yesterday, one had consumption, another one had swelled head, fancied himself a duke to judge by his talk, another was six foot seven or thereabouts, couldn't have taken him aboard without his head sticking out of the saloon hatch, another guy was on a tramp from Oskosh to S'uthern California and wanted to take the expedition *en route*, he was an oil prospector and troubled with something that made him want to scratch; then there was an Italian who'd been a count and an Irishman who'd served in the Irish rebellion under Roger Casement, a decent chap, but I'd just as soon take aboard a live bomb shell. We'll just have to make out, you and me, as after-guard—four Chinks will be enough for a crew and I can pick them up by the handful."

"When are the provisions and stuff coming on board?"

"Tomorrow or next day. I saw J. B. yesterday—"

"*Wear Jack*, ahoy!" came a voice from the wharf through the open skylight.

"Hullo!" cried Hank. "Who's that and what d'you want?"

A thud came on the deck followed by the voice at the companion hatch. "May I come below?" The stairs creaked and at the saloon door appeared a man.

The sun glow from the skylight struck him full as he stood there, a huge, red-bearded, blue-eyed sailor man, neatly dressed in dark serge and wearing a red necktie. His eyes were most taking and astonishing liquid sparkling blue— the eyes of a child.

Contrasted with the hatchet-faced Hank and the sophisticated Bud, he seemed youthful, yet he was older than either of them.

CHAPTER X

THE RED BEARDED ONE

"HULLO!" said Hank. "What the devil do you want?"

"Am I speaking to Mr. Fisher?" asked the newcomer, addressing himself to the town lot speculator.

"You are."

"You're the man that's going after the Dutchman?"

"Yep."

"D'you want to catch him?"

"Oh, Lord, no," said Hank. "I'm only going to inquire after his health. Go on, what are you getting at?"

"Well, if you want to catch him, get on deck this instant minute and see I've not been followed. Go up casual and have a look round. Keep your eyes skinned for a man with a patch over his left eye. I'm not funning. I mean business. Get a-deck. I tell you I've no time to explain."

Hank stared at the other for a second, then he uncoiled himself, crossed the cabin and vanished up the companion way.

Neither George nor the bearded one spoke a word. They were listening. Then they heard voices.

"Say, you," came a voice from the wharf, "did y' see a guy goin' along here—red-whiskered fella?"

"Man with a red necktie?" came Hank's voice.

"Yeh—he's my pal—which way was he goin'?"

"He was making along towards the union dock."

Silence. The companion way creaked and Hank reappeared standing in the cabin doorway.

"Well," said Hank, "that's done. I'd no sooner got on deck than a fellow with a patch on his eye came along with kind inquiries. I've sent him along. Now I must ask you for your visiting card—and explanations."

The stranger laughed.

"Candon's my name," said he. "Bob Candon. I'll take a seat for a minute, if you don't mind, to get my wits together. I only blew in yesterday afternoon, came up from S'uthard and anchored off Tiburon and first news I had when I got ashore was about you and the Dutchman."

"What was your ship?" cut in Hank.

"*Heart of Ireland*, thirty-ton schooner, owned and run by Pat McGinnis, last port—" Candon cut himself short. "That would be telling," said he, with a laugh.

Hank handed him a cigarette and lit another.

"I'm not wanting to bore into your business," said Hank, "only I'm giving you this straight, I've no time for blind man's buff. You were proposing to come along with us to hook the Dutchman?"

"That's what I'm here for," said Candon. "I don't want you to lose wind or time over me, I'd have you know I'm dealing straight, but I'm mixed with a crowd that's not straight, get me? Don't you bother where the *Heart* dropped her mud-hook last, nor how much her business was mixed up with the Dutchman's business. Don't you bother about one single thing but the proposition I'm going to put before you, and it's this. Ship me out of this port down south and I'll put in your hand every last ounce of the boodle the Dutchman's been collecting, for I know where it's hid; on top of that I'll make you a present of the man himself for I know where he's to be found. That's my part of the bargain. And now for yours. I ask nothing but five thousand dollars in my fist when the job's done, and to be put ashore somewhere safe, so that those chaps on the *Heart* won't be able to get at me."

He had been holding the cigarette unlighted. He struck a match, lit it, took in a great volume of smoke and slowly expelled it.

"Well," said he, "what's your opinion on that?"

Hank was sitting almost like Rodin's Thinker. Then he uncoiled a bit.

"Do those guys on the *Heart* know where the Dutchman's to be found?" asked he.

"No, they don't."

"Do they know where the boodle is?"

"N'more than Adam."

"Do they know you know where it is?"

"They suspect. That's my trouble—what's this I'm saying, 'suspect'. Why it's more than that now. Now I've run away from them they'll know for certain."

"And if they catch you?"

"They'll drill me, sure."

"Was that guy with the patch, McGinnis?"

"Nope—Thacker, McGinnis's right hand man."

Hank brooded.

Then said he: "Were you a friend of the Dutchman?"

"What you mean to ask," said the other, "is, am I letting him down? I'll just tell you, the Dutchman has been my enemy, but I'm not moving in this because I have a grouch against him. I'm playing my own game, but it's a straight game."

Hank brooded a second more.

"We'd have to hide you aboard here till we start," said he.

"You will," replied the other.

"Right," said Hank. "Now will you take a rag and clean the engine for two minutes while I have a talk to my friend here in private."

He led the way out and came back.

"Well," said he, "what do you think of that guy?"

"I like him," said George.

"I like him well enough," said Hank, "Question is about his story. It seems plain enough. He's come up with a crew of hoodlums who've been in touch with Vanderdecken, they've been hunting for old man Vanderdecken's boodle. Nothing doing. Then they've left the hunt and put in here. They had big suspicions he was in the know and wanted the boodle for himself. He's only been let ashore with a nurse and he's given her the slip. It's all plain. Then Providence comes in, which is us. Seems extraordinary, don't it? Barrett advertising us like that and all, for here we are, a sure bolt-hole for him, advertised bigger than Heinz's Pickles."

"How do you mean a bolt-hole?"

"Well, look at it. Those crooks are after him like a coyote after a prairie dog. He's got to get out of here, he might get out in a foc'sle if he wasn't knifed before the ship sailed, but that wouldn't lead him anywhere except maybe round Cape Horn, *whereas* he gets a lift back down the coast to where he knows the Dutchman has hid the boodle and he gets five thousand dollars in his fist and a set ashore. Then Providence comes in again, seems to me. I reckoned I'd have to spend five thousand on this expedition and between Tyrebuck and Barrett it won't cost me a cent, bar the hire of four Chinks for crew, so I can easy afford to pay him five thousand and come out winners. Besides, he's an extra hand himself and a good sailor man, if I'm any judge."

"It does seem all to fit in," said George.

"Well, shall we take him?" said Hank. "It's a risk, but I reckon we've got to take risks."

"Take him," said George.

Hank went out and returned with the other. Candon had taken off his coat and his shirt sleeves were rolled up and his hands showed the engine-room business he had been put on.

"Come right in," said Hank. "We've concluded to take you along, but there's conditions."

"Spit them out," said Candon.

"Well, first of all I haven't five thousand dollars to be taking down the coast with me, but I'll put a thousand in your fist when the job's done and mail you the other four to any address you like."

"Oh, I'll trust you for that," said Candon. "What else?"

"Second, if we find the Dutchman's property, it will have to go back to the owners."

"That's just what I'd like best," said Candon. "I tell you straight it would have been a condition with me, only I took it for granted seeing you're out, so to speak, in the name of the law. I'm no pirate. I'm not saying I was always of the same way of thinking, but I reckon those ballyhooleys I've just left have given me a shake."

"Well then," said Hank, "there's only one more condition. You'll help to work the ship for your bunk and board without pay."

"Right," said Candon, "and now, if you'll take that styleographic pen I see sticking out of your vest pocket and give's a bit of paper, we'll draw the contract."

Hank produced the pen and an old bill on the back of which the "contract" was made out, under the terms of which Candon was to receive five thousand dollars and a set ashore after the Dutchman had been brought safe aboard the *Wear Jack*, also he was to take the expedition to the spot where, to the best of his belief, was cached the Dutchman's plunder.

This done, Candon went back to his engine cleaning, having produced and handed over to Hank four ten dollar notes.

"I'll want a toothbrush and a couple of shirts and a couple of suits of pyjamas," said he. "Maybe, as I can't get ashore, you'll get them for me. All my truck's on board the *Heart*."

"Bud," said Hank to his partner that night, "I hope to the Lord we ain't stung. Suppose the chap's some practical joker put on us by Barrett, or the boys at the Club."

"Nonsense," said George. "Where'd be the sense? Besides the chap's genuine. You have only to look at his face...."

CHAPTER XI

NIGHT

THE week before the sailing of the *Wear Jack* was a busy time for the Fisher Syndicate and business was not expedited owing to the fact that Candon had to be kept hidden. The red-bearded one seemed happy enough, spending most of his time in the engine room smoking cigarettes. At nights, safe with Hank in the "saloon," his mind disclosed itself in his conversation.

No, this was no wasp let in on them by Barrett or the Club boys. The mind of Candon, as revealed to Hank, was as free from crookedness as the eyes through which it looked, and on most topics from the League of Nations to Ella Wheeler Wilcox, it was sound. And it was not unlike the mind of Hank. It was self-educated and their enthusiasms, from the idea of Universal Brotherhood to the idea of the sanctity of womanhood, matched, mostly.

Candon, from what one could gather, had been a rolling stone, like Hank, but he gave little away about himself and he was quite frank about it.

"I'd just as soon forget myself," said he. "I've been in a good many mix-ups and I've missed a fortune twice through my own fault, but I've come through with all my teeth and no stomach worries and we'll leave it at that."

Barrett's stores came on board and were stowed, and Hank, through a boarding-house keeper, got his crew, four Chinamen all of the same tong, all Lees, and bossed by a gentleman rejoicing in the name of Lee Wong Juu. Champagne Charley, Hank labeled him. They came tripping on board with their chests the night before starting, vanished like shades down the foc'sle hatch and were seen no more.

Hank, standing on the deck with George, heaved a sigh of contentment. "Well, that's done," said he. "There's nothing more to take on board and we're all ready for the pull out in the morning."

"What time do you propose to start?" asked the other.

"Sunup. Barrett has got it into his head, somehow, we're going at noon. I didn't tell you, but I got wind he'd arranged for a tug with a brass band to lead us out and josh us. Can you see his face when he finds us gone?"

They went below where the cabin lamp was lit, with Candon reading a newspaper under it.

"The Chinks are come," said Hank, taking his seat at the table, and fetching out his pipe. "There's nothing more to come in but the mud-hook. Well, how do you feel, now we're starting?"

"Bully," said Candon. "I was beginning to feel like a caged canary. You chaps don't know what it's been the last week. Well, let's get finished. There's some truck still to be stowed in the after cabin and I want to do a bit more tinkering at the engine. There's a day's work on that engine—them cylinder rings were sure made in Hades."

"Well, you can leave it," said Hank. "I'm putting out at sunup. I don't count on that engine and you'll have time to tinker with her on the way down." He stopped suddenly, raised his head, and held up a finger. The night was warm and the skylight full open. In the dead silence that fell on the cabin they could hear through the open skylight the far-away rattle of a cargo winch working under the electrics, the whistle of a ferry boat and away, far away, though great as the voice of Behemoth, the boo of a deep sea steamer's siren.

"Yes," began Hank again, gliding to the door of the saloon as he spoke, "you can tinker with it on the way down." He vanished, and the others, taking his cue, kept up the talk. Then they heard him pounce.

"What you doing here?"

"Hullo! me—I ain't doin' nothin'—what you gettin' at? You lea' me go."

"What you doing here, you low down scow-hunker? Answer up before I scrag you."

"Tell you I was doin' nothin'. I dropped aboard to see if I couldn't borry a light, seein' the shine of your skylight."

"I'll give you a light."

Then they heard the quite distinctive sounds of a man being kicked off the ship, blasphemous threats from the wharf-side—silence.

A minute later Hank appeared, his lean face lit with the light of battle.

"Popped my head on deck," cried Hank, "and saw a fellow on the wharf-side—I'll swear it was Jake. He lit, and then I saw another one hunched down by the skylight. You heard me kicking him off."

"Who's Jake?" asked Candon, who had taken his seat again at the table.

"Watchman I fired for handing me lies more'n a fortnight ago."

"Well," said Candon, "the other man was Mullins, if I have my ears on my head."

"Who's Mullins?"

"Black Mullins, McGinnis' left hand. Boys, we've gotta get out. How's the wind?"

"Nor'west," said Hank.

"And there's a moon. Boys, we've gotta get right out now, get the whaleboat over and the Chinks ready for a tow clear of the wharf. Let's see, the whole of the *Heart* crowd will be over at Tiburon, the old *Heart* will be in dry dock, for she'd started a butt and there's weeks' work on her, so they won't be able to use her to chase us for another fortnight, get me? Well, see now, that guy will be back in Tiburon somewhere about two hours or more and he'll rouse the hive. He'll have seen me, lookin' down through the skylight, and he'll know you're starting to-morrow. Not having a ship to chase us, they'll board us. You'll have a boatload of gunmen alongside somewhere about two in the morning."

"You mean to say they'll board us?" cried George.

"Yep."

"But what about the police?"

"Police! Nothing. Why they'd beat it in a quick launch before the cops had begun to remember they weren't awake."

"Well, let's notify the police and have an ambush ready for them."

"Not me," said Candon. "I don't want to have any dealings with the law. Why if McGinnis and his crowd were taken, they'd swear Lord knows what about me. Besides I'm not friends with the bulls. I'm no crook, I've never looked inside a jail, but I've seen enough good men done in by the law to make me shy of it."

"But see here," said Hank. "I can't take her out at night. I don't know the lights, I'd pile her up sure."

"I'll take her out," said Candon, "I'd take her out with my eyes shut. It's near full moon and we'll have the ebb, what more do you want?"

Hank turned to George.

"Let's get out," said George. "We don't want a mix-up with those people; if we get piled, why we have the boat."

Hank turned to Candon.

"You're sure you can do it?"

"Sure."

"Then come on," said Hank. He led the way on deck.

The wharf was deserted. To the left of them lay the bay, silver under the moonlight and spangled here and there with the lights of shipping at anchor. Whilst Hank trimmed the side lights and Candon attended to the binnacle light, George went forward to rout out the Chinks. He found them finishing their supper. Lee Wong Juu was their cook as well as boss, he had lit the galley stove on his own initiative and made tea. They had brought provisions enough for supper. Their chests were arranged in order, everything was in apple-pie trim and as they sat on their bunk sides with their tin mugs in their hands and their glabrous faces slewed round on the intruder, they looked not unlike a company of old maids at a tea party.

George gave his order and they rose, put away their mugs and followed him on deck.

The whaleboat had cost Hank ninety-five dollars, second-hand. It was not a real whaleboat, either in size, make or fittings, but good enough for their purpose, carvel built, four-oared, with tins fixed beneath the thwarts to help float her in case of a capsize.

Candon was standing by the boat as George came on deck.

In the rapid moments that had come on them since the spy had been kicked off the ship, Candon had gradually gained supremacy, without effort, one might say. The man had arisen and was rising to the emergency like a swimmer on a wave, bearing the others with him. He was giving orders now quietly and without fuss.

They got the boat afloat with the four Chinks in her, and, the tow rope having been fixed, Candon got into her, having cast off the mooring ropes. Hank took the wheel of the schooner. George, standing silent beside Hank, heard the creak and splash of the oars. Then came the chug and groan of the tow-rope tightening, then slowly, almost imperceptibly the bowsprit of the *Wear Jack* began to veer away from the wharf. And now to port and starboard lay the glittering harbour water and astern the long line of the wharves began to show with the electrics blazing here and there where they were working cargo overtime. As the wharves receded, they stole into a world of new sounds and lights. San Francisco began to show her jewelry, glittering ribbons of electrics, crusts of gems; on the port bow the lights of Oakland, far across the water, answered to the lights of San Francisco, and across the scattered silver ferry boats showed like running jewels. The wind from the north west came steady and filled with the breath of the unseen sea.

"Lord!" said Hank, "how much further is he taking us? Seems like as if he were making for Oakland."

"He knows what he is doing," said George.

"Sure."

They held on.

A Chinese junk passed, with her lateen sail bellying to the wind, and then came along a yacht, lighted and riotous as a casino, with a jazz band playing "Suwanee." It passed and the great quietude of the night resumed. Still the tow kept on.

Then came a voice from alongside. Candon had cast off the rope and was coming on board.

To George, just in that moment, the whole scene and circumstance came as an impression never to be forgotten; the silence following the casting off of the rope, the vast harbour surface, glittering like a ball-room floor, where the helpless *Wear Jack* lay adrift, the lights of 'Frisco and the lights of Oakland and the secrecy and necessity for despatch lest, drifting as they were, they should be side-swiped by some Bay boat in a hurry. But he had little time for thought. Candon was on board, the boat was got in and the slack of the tow-rope, and Candon at the wheel began to give his orders with speed but without hurry.

The mainsail rose slatting against the stars, then the foresail; a Chink cast the gaskets off the jib, whilst the *Wear Jack*, trembling like an undecided and frightened thing, seemed to calm down and take heart. The slatting of the canvas ceased. They were under way.

Candon seemed steering for Oakland, then the Oakland lights swung to starboard and passed nearly astern. They were making for Alcatraz. The lights of San Francisco were now to port and the city showed immense, heaving itself against the moonlight; Nobs Hill, Telegraph Hill, Russian Hill, all ablaze beneath the moon, slashed with lines of light. Away beyond Angel Island showed the lights of Tiburon.

Right under Alcatraz, Candon put the helm hard over; the canvas thrashed and filled again and the *Wear Jack* settled down on her new tack, heading for the Presidio. Close in, the helm went over again, the canvas fought the wind and then filled on the tack for Lime Point, the northern gate post of the Golden Gate.

The breath of the sea now came strong, spray came inboard from the meeting of wind and ebb tide and the *Wear Jack* began to thrash at the tumble coming in from the bar.

Under Lime Point she came about on the port tack, taking the middle passage. Then beyond Pont Bonito came the tumble of the bar. The wind was not more than a steady sailing breeze but the long rollers coming in from Japan gave them all the trouble they wanted, though the *Wear Jack*, proving her good qualities, shipped scarcely a bucket full. Then the sea smoothed down to a glassy breeze-spangled swell and the schooner, with the loom of the land far on her port quarter, spread her wings beneath the moon for the south.

CHAPTER XII

OUT

CANDON handed the wheel over to Hank. "Well, we're out," said he. "Keep her as she goes, the coast's a straight line down to Point San Pedro, and I don't want to clear it by more than ten miles." He lit a pipe and walked to the port rail, where he stood with the pipe in his mouth and his hands on the rail looking at the land.

George stood beside him. The crew had vanished to the foc'sle, now that everything was comfortable, leaving the deck to the three white men; no watches had been picked nor was there a look-out. George remarked on the fact and Candon laughed.

"I'd just as soon leave the Chinks below," said he, "and run her ourselves for the rest of the watch. Half a man could handle her as the wind is, and as for a look-out, why I reckon nothing could sink us to-night. Boys, I'm sure bughouse, I never took a ship out of 'Frisco bay before two hours ago."

"You what!" said George.

"What I'm telling you. It came on me to do it and I did it. I've been in and out often enough, but never at the wheel nor navigating. I had the lay of the place in my head but it was a near touch."

Hank at the wheel gave a laugh that sounded like a cough.

"I felt it in my bones," said Hank.

"What?" asked Candon.

"Why that you were driving out half blind; as near as paint you had us on to Alcatraz and you all but rammed the Presidio. I was standing on my toes wanting to yell 'Put your helm over,' but I kept my head shut, didn't want to rattle you."

"Bughouse, clean bughouse," said Candon. "Makes me sweat in the palms of my hands now I've done it, but I tell you boys, I couldn't have missed. Going by night like that one can't judge distance and as for the lights, they'd better have been away, but I couldn't have missed, I was so certain sure of myself. It comes on me like that at times, I get lifted above myself, somehow or another."

"I'm the same way myself," said Hank, "it comes on me as if I got light-headed and I'm never far wrong if I let myself go. Bud here will tell you I rushed this expedition through more by instinct than anything else—didn't I, Bud?"

Bud assented, unenthusiastically.

George Harley du Cane, out and away now with the Pacific beneath him and his eyes fixed on the far-off loom of the land, was thinking. He had recognized, even before starting, that Hank and Candon were, temperamentally, pretty much birds of the same feather. Not only had their discussions as to socialism and so forth seemed to him pretty equally crazy, but he had recognized, in a dim sort of manner, that they infected one another and that their "bughouse" qualities were not diminished by juxtaposition. However, safe in port, the sanity or insanity of his companions, expressed only in conversation about abstract and uninteresting affairs, did not seem to matter. Out here it was different, somehow, especially after the exhibition Candon had just given them of daring carried to the limits of craziness. And who was Candon, anyhow? A likable man, sure enough, but the confessed associate of more than shady characters, and they had accepted this man on his face value, as a pilot in an adventure that was sure to be dangerous, considering the character of the man they were out to hunt.

Well, there was not a bit of use bothering. He had gone into the business with his eyes open. There he was, wealthy, at ease with all the world, talking to those men in the club, when in came Hank with his lunacy, saying he was going to catch Vanderdecken. He had followed the Rat Trap Inventor out, taken his arm and insisted on becoming part and parcel of his plans. Why? He could not tell why. And now he was tied up in a venture with Chinks and two cranks; a venture which, if it failed, would make him ridiculous, if it succeeded might make him a corpse. He might now have been respectably shooting in the Rockies only for his own stupidity.

Then, all of a sudden, came a question to his mind, "Would you sooner be respectably shooting in the Rockies or here?" Followed by the surprising and immediate answer, "Here." Bughouse—clean bughouse—but the fact remained.

It was now getting on for two in the morning, and he went below, leaving the deck to the others. They intended carrying on till four, and then rousing the crew up for the morning watch.

They told him they would call him when they wanted him and he turned in, dropping to sleep the instant his head touched the pillow. When he awoke it was daylight, water dazzles were at play on the Venesta panellings, as the early sunlight through the portholes shifted to the lift of the swell, snores from the two other occupied bunks seemed to keep time to the movement of the *Wear Jack* and from the topmost starboard bunk, Hank's pyjama-clad leg hung like the leg of a dead man.

The whole of the after-guard had turned in, leaving apparently the schooner to run herself. He turned out and without stopping to wake the others came hurriedly up the companion way on deck.

CHAPTER XIII

THE BAY OF WHALES

THE sun was up and away to port lay California, lifting her hills to heaven against the morning splendour, to starboard, a mile or so away, a big freighter, in ballast and showing the kick of her propeller, was pounding along north with the sunlight on her bridge canvas. Even at that distance George could hear the thud of her screw like the beating of a heart.

A Chinaman was at the helm of the *Wear Jack*, Champagne Charley no less, and forward another celestial was emptying a slush tub over the port rail.

George nodded to the helmsman, and then, taking his seat on the skylight edge, contemplated the coast.

George's yachting experience had been mainly confined to the Bay. He could steer a boat under sail, but of deep sea work and cruising in big yachts he knew practically nothing. Still, even to his uninitiated mind, this thing seemed wrong. Candon and Hank had evidently left the deck at the beginning of the morning watch, that is to say four o'clock, leaving the Chinks to run the show. They had been running it for three hours or so and doing it satisfactorily, to all appearances. Still it didn't seem right.

He determined to go for the other two and give them a piece of his mind and then, when, a few minutes later, they came on deck yawning and arrayed in their pyjamas, he didn't. They seemed so perfectly satisfied with themselves and things in general that it was beyond him to start complaining. Instead he went down and tubbed in the bathroom. An hour later, as he was seated at breakfast with the two others, his whole attitude of mind towards "Chinks" had changed, for the schooner was running on her course with scarcely a tremor of the tell-tale compass, the breakfast was set as if by a parlour-maid, and the ham and eggs were done to perfection. More than that, they were waited upon by a waiter who knew his business, for when he had done handing things round, he vanished without a word and left them to talk.

"Oh, that's nothing," said Candon, in reply to a remark of George's. "Those Chinks could run this packet by themselves. When a Chinaman signs on as an A. B., he is one. He doesn't pretend to be what he isn't, not on a ship running out of 'Frisco anyhow, and he's more, every Chinaman's a cook and a laundress and it's ten to one he's a tailor as well. I tell you, when I think of what one Chink can do and what one white man generally can't, I get frightened for the whites." Hank was cutting in, and an argument on the colour question between these two was prevented only by George remembering something of more immediate moment.

"Look here," said he to Candon, "can't you tell us more about Vanderdecken now we're out. What I mean to say is the plans you have about him. Where are we going, anyway?"

"South," said Candon.

"I know that," said George, "but where south? South's a big place."

"It is," said the other; "too big for guessing, but now we're out and I'm going to put you wise. First of all, I promised you to put this guy's boodle into your hands, and second I promised you the guy himself. I hung off from telling you the location till you'd done your part of the contract and got me out away from the McGinnis crowd. Well, you've done your part and here's mine. The place I'm taking you is known by the Mexicans as the Bay of Whales."

"The Mexicans!" said George.

"Yep. We've got to turn the corner of Lower California, that's to say Cape St. Lucas, then out across the Bay of California for the Mexican coast and the Bay of Whales. It's away above Jalisco. It's worth seeing. I don't know how it is, maybe it's the currents or the winds or just a liking for a quiet burying ground, but every old sulphur bottom that's died between here and Timbuctoo seems to have laid his bones there. There's a Mexican superstition about the place, maybe on account of the bones, but no one ever goes there. It's the lonesomest place on God's footstool, the shore-along ships keep clear of it and it's all reefs beyond the sand of the bay so you don't get ships putting in. I tell you, you could photograph the lonesomeness. Well there the boodle is and there you'll put your hands on the guy you want."

Said Hank: "Look here, B. C."—Candon had come down to initials after the manner of 'Frisco. "How did old man Vanderdecken make out, anyway. What I'm getting at is this: I figured his fishing grounds to be the Channel Islands and north and south of there, but that's a good long way from St. Lucas."

"That's so," said Candon. "Well, I'll tell you, right along till near the end he used to keep the stuff he got aboard his own hooker. You're right, his lay was the Channel Islands. But finding he'd made the place too hot for himself all right along down the American seaboard, and expectin' to be searched, he did a dive for the bay I told you of and there he cached the stuff, and I'm the only man beside himself that knows where the cache is.

"There, I've told you that much. I'm not going to say how I got so thick with him as to know his plans and dispositions. I just ask you to take B. C.'s word that the goods are according to the manifest."

"Oh, that's all right," said Hank, "I don't want to dig into your business, all I want's the Dutchman, and to put my hand on his shoulder."

"And so you shall," said B. C., "'less he dies before we get there."

They came up and, Candon taking the wheel, the two Chinamen who were holding the deck dived below. An hour later, the Chinks being called up, watches were picked, George falling to Hank, Champagne Charley to Candon.

Candon being the most knowledgeable man and the best sailor, it was agreed that he should work the ship.

"You can't have two heads," said Hank, "and I reckon yours is better than mine where navigating her is concerned."

CHAPTER XIV

ST. NICOLAS

THE Kuro Shiwo current drives northward up the coast of Japan, crosses the Pacific and comes down the Pacific Coast of America, bathing the Channel Islands and giving them their equable temperature. This great current is a world of its own; it has its kelp forests, where the shark hides, like a tiger, and its own peculiar people, led by the great swordfish of Japan. Japan not only sends her swordsmen of the sea to keep this moving street-like world, she lends her colours, in blues vivid and surprising as the skies and waters of her shadowless pictures.

One morning, shortly after sunrise, George, fast asleep in his bunk, was hauled out by Hank to "see the Islands." He tumbled out and, just as he was, in his pyjamas, followed on deck.

Between the Kuro Shiwo and the wind the *Wear Jack* was making a good ten knots. Pont Concepcion on the mainland lay almost astern, and the sun, with his feet still on the mountains beyond Santa Barbara, was chasing to death a fog whose last banners were fluttering amidst the foot hills.

Away ahead, like vast ships under press of sail, rode the San Lucas Islands, San Miguel, Santa Rosa, Santa Cruz, their fog-filled cañons white in the sunlight.

Later in the morning, with the San Lucas Islands far astern, San Nicolas showed up like a flake of spar on the horizon to the south; to the sou'-east appeared a trace of the mountains of Santa Catalina.

Candon, who was on deck talking to George, pointed towards Santa Catalina. "Looks pretty lonely, don't it?" said he. "Well, that place is simply swarming with millionaires. Say, you're something in that way yourself, aren't you? So I ought to keep my head muzzled, but you'll understand. I'm not going against you, but things in general. I reckon if you'd ever roomed in Tallis Street, 'Frisco, you'd know what I mean. I've seen big poverty and when I see millionaires sunning themselves, it gets my goat—now you know what I'm gettin' at."

"Look here, B. C.," said George, "cut it out. Most of the millionaires I know live on pap and pills and work like gun mules—"

"Do you?" asked Candon laughing.

"No, I don't, but I expect I will some time; anyhow, one fool exception doesn't count. What I'm getting at is this, chaps like you and Hank get it in your heads that the bigger a man's pile is, the more he enjoys himself. It's the other way about, seems to me; also that the rich man lives in a world of his own with laws of his own—"

"So he does," said the other. "Now you listen to me. When Prohibition started, how did the poor man stand? Dry, that's how he stood, looking at the other people with their cellars full of drink. They knew the law was coming and they laid in."

"That's true," said George.

"It is," said Candon, "and some day, maybe, I'll tell you a yarn about how it hit me once."

Hank came on deck and stood with eyes shaded, looking at the ghost of Santa Catalina on the sky line. "There she is," said Hank. "You can almost see the flags waving and hear the bands playing. Bud, didn't you ever go fishing down that way? I reckon it was that place gave Vanderdecken his first pull towards thievery, seeing the water is thick with Bank Presidents and Wheat Cornerers only waiting to be collected for ransom. Say, B. C., if you know anything about old Vanderdecken, tell us why he didn't hold the folks he caught to ransom as well as picking the diamonds and money off them. That's what I'd have done. I would sure. Hullo!"

A leaping tuna, as long as a man and curved like a sword, left the sea on the starboard bow, showed its colours to the sun, and vanished with a splash.

"Tuna," said Candon.

"Well, what's he doing here?" asked Hank, "he's out of his waters, this ain't the tuna grounds."

"How do you know?" asked George.

"Lord, oughtn't I to know," replied Hank. "Why I was on the fish commission ship on this section of the Pacific Coast, sounding and dredging and taking specimens of the fish and the weeds and Lord knows what all. That was five years ago, but I reckon the tuna grounds haven't altered since then."

"They lie south of San Clemente, don't they?" said Candon.

"They do not, you're thinking of albacore. The tuna grounds are east of Santa Catalina mostly, close to Avalon. Why, I know all that place's well as I know my own office. I've got a hellnation memory for facts and I could reel off to you the lie of the fishing grounds most all along the coast. Right from Rocky Point on the mainland the fish begin running in shoals. Benito you get mostly at Rocky Point, then albacore; but if you strike out for the Islands you'll begin to get big things."

"Whales?" asked George.

"Whales mostly stick to the Santa Barbara channel, there aren't many now, but you get killers and sulphur bottoms and gray whales—sharks, too."

Hank lit a cigarette and leaning on the port rail looked across the water to the east. Then he came forward a bit and looked ahead.

Away ahead and a bit to westward something showed. It was San Nicolas, San Nicolas no longer sharply defined like a flame of spar, but with its head in a turban of new-formed cloud. This island, eight or nine miles long, forms the western outpost of the Channel Islands. Unprotected, like them, by Port Concepcion, it receives the full force of wind and weather.

The others came close to Hank.

"That's her," said Hank, "that's San Nicolas. Ever been ashore there, B. C.?"

"Not such a fool," said Candon. "I've cruised about these waters a good bit, but I've never met a man who wanted to put his foot there. It's all wind and sand for one thing."

"Well," said Hank, "I've been thinking, from what I know of the place, that Vanderdecken may have used San Nicolas for one of his ports of call. What do you say, B. C.?"

"Who knows?" said Candon.

"Did you land on San Nicolas?" asked George.

"Oh yes; we were hanging off the kelp beds three or four days."

"I'd like to land there," said George.

"Well, it's easily done," said Hank. "We could tie up the kelp for the matter of that, only I'm afraid the *Wear Jack's* a bit too big. She might drag out. Away down, further south, the kelp vines run to a thousand foot long and you could most moor a battleship to them, but it's different here. However, we can anchor if you want to. What do you say, B. C.?"

"I'm with you," said Candon. "We have plenty of time and a day won't matter."

"Not a cent," said George.

Candon went and leaned on the starboard rail. For the last two days, in fact, ever since he had given away the whereabouts of Vanderdecken's cache, he had seemed at times depressed. Sometimes he would be in high good spirits and sometimes moping and silent. Hank had noticed it first and he spoke of it now as he and George went forward to the bow, where they hung watching the boost of the water and the foam gouts like marble shavings on lazalite.

"Notice B. C. has the dumps again," said Hank. "I wonder what's working on him? Maybe he feels himself a skunk leading us on to old man Vanderdecken."

"He said that was all right," said George, "said he was acting perfectly straight and that the man was his enemy. Y'know, I believe in B. C."

"So do I," said Hank, "but what in the nation's he moulting about, that's what I want to know. I take it it's just sensitiveness; even though the Dutchman is his enemy, he don't like giving him away. I can understand it."

"I can't quite make him out," said George, "he's intelligent and has fine ideas about things, yet he always seems to have lived pretty rough—"

"And what's the harm of that," cut in Hank. "Why, it's the guys that have lived pretty rough as you call it that are the only educated citizens as far as I can make out. They've had their noses rubbed into the world. Why look at me—I'm not saying I'm much, but all I've learned of any good to me hasn't come out of class-rooms or colleges. Mind you, I'm not against them, I don't say they're no use, but I do say what makes a man is what he rubs against."

"He seems to have been rubbing against some pretty queer characters to judge by the *Heart of Ireland* lot," said George.

"That's my point," said Hank. "They've turned him respectable. There's many a man would have gone to the bad only he's been frightened off it by the toughs he's met. They're better than Sunday school books. I know, for I've been there."

An hour later, San Nicolas was plain before them and an hour before sunset Beggs Rock was on the starboard bow and only a mile away. San Nicolas, itself close to them, now showed its peak, nine hundred feet high with its changeless turban of cloud, rosy gold in the evening glow. From the peak the island spilled away showing cleft and cañon and high ground treeless and devoid of life.

They cast anchor just outside the kelp ring. The sun was just leaving the sea. Nothing showed but the brown lateen sails of a Chinese junk, standing in shore about two miles away. She rounded a promontory and vanished from sight.

"That's a Chow fishing boat," said Hank. "They go scraping along all down this coast, hunting for abalones and turtle and whatever they can lay their hands on."

"That's so," said Candon, "I've met in with them right down to the Gulf of California and beyond. It's against the law to take abalones in most places round here, but much they care."

"They'd lay hands on any old thing," said Hank. "Wonder what that crowd is doing here?"

The morrow was to tell him.

CHAPTER XV

WHAT THE CHINKS WERE DOING

THEY had fixed to row ashore after breakfast but fishing held them till afternoon. Candon, not keen on the business of climbing over rocks, remained behind to finish tinkering at the engine which he had almost got into working order.

Usually there is a big swell running here, but to-day there was only a gentle heave lifting the long green vine tendrils of the kelp. It was like rowing over a forest. On the beach they left the boat to the two Chinamen who had rowed them off and, Hank leading the way, they started to the right towards the great sand spit that runs into the sea for half a mile or more.

A Farallone cormorant, circling in the blue above, seemed to watch them; it passed with a cry, leaving the sky empty and nothing to hear but the wash of the sea on the beaches and far off an occasional gull's voice from the spit. Reaching a great forward leaning rock, they took their seats in the shade of it to rest and light their pipes. The sand lay before them, jutting into the kelp-oily sea and beyond the kelp the blue of the kuro shiwo. The *Wear Jack* was out of sight, the horizon seemed infinitely far and of a world where men were not or from whence men had departed for ever.

"Say, Bud," said Hank, leaning on his side with a contented sigh, "ain't this great!"

"Which?" asked Bud.

"The lonesomeness. Listen to the gulls, don't they make you feel just melancholy."

"Do you like to feel melancholy?"

"Depends on the brand, same as whisky. Say, it's funny to think that the cars are running down Market Street and Tyrebuck sitting in his office and J. B.—he's sitting at his luncheon by this. Wonder what they said when they found us gone? Well we've had the laugh on them to start with."

"I hope they won't have the laugh on us at the finish," said George.

"Don't," said Hank, "it makes me feel doddery to think of us going back like dogs with our tails down and no Dutchman—hell! no, you don't see me back in 'Frisco empty-handed, never. Was you ever laughed at, Bud?"

"Heaps of times."

"Laughed at in the papers?"

"No."

"Well, that's what I mean. I've been, and I know."

"What was the business?"

"Oh, it was a girl."

"What did she do?"

"It wasn't what she did so much as what she said. It was this way. I was in Pittsburg one rainy day and I fell in with a girl; she wasn't more'n eighteen and down on her luck. She asked me the way to somewhere or another and that's how we started off. She'd had nothing to eat that day and I took her into a coffee shop and stuffed her up with buckwheat cakes and truck and then she told me her story. Said she had to meet her father at the station that evening and he was old and infirm and they had to look for rooms. Well, it seems, somehow or another, I was mug enough to help her look for rooms and stand as a reference and lend her twenty dollars, and when the police stepped into the rooms I got for them that night and took the grey wig and patch over his eye off her father he was Sam Brown, the biggest tough out of N' York, with five thousand dollars' worth of stolen diamonds on him. I managed to clear myself, but the press had got the story and I tell you, Bud, I was guyed out of Pittsburg and it hurt worse than kicking."

"They don't go in for sentiment in Pittsburg."

"Nope, steel goods."

"Well, come along," said George, "this isn't prospecting the island."

They got up and shook the sand from themselves and started along the spit; then, returning, they began to climb. The *Wear Jack* came into view, anchored beyond the kelp, then as they got higher and above the promontory that hid the next bay, they saw the Chinese junk of the night before. She was anchored a little way out. On the sands of the bay stood three strange looking little pyramids, tents evidently, and about the tents people were moving.

"Now what in the nation are those Chinks doing?" said Hank. He unslung his binoculars he had brought with him and leveled them at the far-off tents.

"Chinks—one of them's building a fire; they've got a boat up on the sand. Abalone hunters, most likely, making a camp here for the fishing. Say, Bud, I believe they're hatchet men."

"What are hatchet men?"

"Pirates turned inside out and painted to look like fishermen—just robbers, abalone poachers and smugglin' if they can get a chance, wickedest lot out of hell,—I'm judging by the look of them. Have a squint."

He handed the powerful glasses to George who leveled them in the direction of the bay.

The field of sight suddenly swarmed with Chinamen moving against the glitter of white sand. Small, dingy-looking men, wearing big straw hats,—a fire had been lit and the white smoke curled upwards against the tents. Near one of the tents a Chinaman was working over a heap of what looked like abalones.

"Hullo!" cried George.

"What's up?" asked Hank.

"There's a white man with them, he's just come out of one of the tents—a long thin looking devil. What on earth's he with them for?"

Hank took the glass.

"Sure enough there is," said Hank, "look at his hair all hanging over his face. He looks to be bossing the Chinks. It's plain now what they are. Smugglers, opium or dope of some sort. I've heard the trade's in the hands of whites, they run it into Santa Barbara plugged into abalone shells. Bud! Say! Bud! There's a girl! She's just come out of the right-hand tent with a little chap after her, looks like a Mexican. She's a white—looks like a lady—she's crying, she's got her handkerchief to her face—Bud, this gets me!"

George snatched the glass.

Hank was right. There was a girl amidst the horrid crowd. She was no longer crying, she had taken her seat on the sand in a dejected sort of manner and seemed watching the others as they moved about at their work. Even at that distance, it was obvious that she was of a different class from the rest.

"Well, I'm damned," said George.

"Look! that beastly big chap seems jawing at her." Hank snatched the glass.

He saw the long man standing in front of the girl whom he seemed to have ordered to her feet; he seemed angry about something. Then the unfortunate girl turned and went off towards one of the tents. She seemed about to enter it when she collapsed, cast herself on the sand and lay, her face hidden on her arm.

"Hell!" cried Hank.

He shut the glass, thrust it into its case and started off down the rocks, George following.

"Where are you going to?" cried George.

"Bust up that hive," cried Hank. "That's white slave, clean white slave. Come along to the ship and fetch Candon and the guns. This is better than Vanderdecken."

Tumbling, slipping, clawing at bushes, whooping like a red Indian, he led the way, George labouring behind, till they reached the beach where the boat of the *Wear Jack* lay, the two Chinks close by it on the sand, smoking and playing fan-tan. The boat was shoved off.

"You mean fighting them?" asked George. His throat was dry and his lips were dry. He had seen the Great War and bursting shells and had risked his life a dozen times, but all that seemed nothing to the imminent attack on that horrid crowd over there on the beach beyond sight.

"Oh, Lord, no," said Hank, a devilish look on his lantern face, and a new light in his eyes. "I'm going to cuddle them. Lay into it, you jade-faced sons of perdition. 'Nuff! in with your oars and claw on."

They tumbled over the rail of the *Wear Jack*, Hank shouting for Candon. They found him below coming out of the engine place with a lump of cotton waste in his hand.

"Come into the saloon," cried Hank. "B. C., we're up to the eyes in it. Wacha think, we've struck a gang of Chinese white slavers with a girl in tow." He explained.

As he talked, George noticed the effect on Candon. He leaned forward as he sat, pulling at the hairs of his beard; his eyes changed in colour, darkening as the pupils spread. When Hank had finished, Candon leaned back, sought mechanically in his pocket, found his pipe and put it between his teeth, but he did not light it.

"They're white slavers," said Hank.

"Sure," said Candon. The anger consuming him was no less visible for the calm that covered it. Then he broke out. "There you have things as they're going on, and your beautiful laws, where are they? I tell you, boys, white women are being snatched off to China every week that goes, and white men are helping. It's all part of a business mixed up with opium smuggling and dope selling. Well, we've gotta get that girl from them. Question is, how?"

"Land right away and go for them. I've got the guns," said Hank, going to a locker and producing the armaments for the voyage, three Lugger automatics. "Here's the persuaders and the Chinks will help."

"One minute," said Candon. He was thinking hard, nearly biting through the pipe stem. Then he spoke. "It's getting on for sun-down. Better wait till the dark comes, then we can rush them. They'll think it's the police if we do it proper and they won't be able to count our numbers—how's the wind?"

"Dropped dead."

"Good, there's no fear of them putting out before we fix them, they'll stay here to-night, sure. Once we get the girl on board, we can put off, wind or no wind, for I've got the engine fixed. You see, if we put up a fight right away we'll have all those Chinks they have with them on top of us. You said they were hatchet men, didn't you? Fight like hornets; whereas in the dark—why a Chink in the dark is no good, specially if he doesn't know what's attacking him. Now, my plan is, bust their camp up sudden, yelling and shooting over them; if they show fight, drill them, but it's a thousand to one they'll quit and scatter, thinking it's the police. Nail the girl, get her aboard here and shove off."

"I'm with you," said George.

Hank demurred for a moment; he would have preferred to attack right away; then, after a little discussion, he fell in with the others.

CHAPTER XVI

EVIDENCE OF CONTRABAND

THEY came on deck.

It wanted little more than two hours to sunset and the eastern sky had taken that look of distance which only comes when the sun is low in the west.

Hank, who was the first on deck, called to the others and pointed over the sea. Something white was shearing through the water over there, something that showed up at once through the glass as a high power motor launch.

"Boys," cried Hank, "it's the police, it's the cops sure as certain, and we're done out of it."

Candon took the glass.

"Don't look like a police boat to me," said he, "and I only see two fellows on her. Of course, there may be a dozen hid away. Looks more like to me that it's a contrabander done up as a pleasure launch. We can't see anything from here. Let's take the boat and push out so that we can get a sight of the next bay."

"They'll spot us," said Hank.

"They'll spot the *Wear Jack* anyhow," said Candon. "The boat doesn't matter, they'll think we're fishing."

The boat was still alongside. Led by Candon, they got in and pushed off.

Half a mile out the next bay had opened enough to show them the junk at anchor and the tents on the beach. The launch, the blue water shearing from her forefoot, was approaching the junk.

Hank, watching through the glass, reported: "They're clawing on. There's only one Chink on the junk, he's handing over parcels and taking things aboard. You're right, B. C., it's no police affair; it's contraband sure enough. Bend over the gunnel, you two, and pretend to be fishing. Now the launch is putting off back to the coast. Well, that settles it."

"Where are they out from?" said Hank.

"Oh, Santa Barbara," said Candon, "sure thing."

They watched the launch making back to the coast, then they took to the oars and put back for the schooner.

"Well," said George, who was at the yoke lines, "it gets me how these sorts of things are let pass by the law."

"Oh, that's nothing," said Hank, with a laugh. "Why, girls are disappearing every week in 'Frisco, they get inveigled into Chinatown and that's all. They get taken off to Canton and sold as slaves to mandarins or worse."

"But how do the Chinks manage to get them out of America?" asked George.

"You've seen it," said Candon. "You said there were two white men with those Chinese—that's how. The traffic wouldn't stand a minute without the help of whites. Money, that's what's the mischief, money and the damned capitalistic system that makes money king. Lord, I want to get at those chaps, I'm sufferin' to get at those chaps." He stopped rowing. Hank, equally excited, also rested on his oar till George cut in and they resumed.

CHAPTER XVII

THE SURPRISE

THEY came alongside the *Wear Jack* just as the fires of sunset began to pale beyond the peak of San Nicolas.

"Come down below, boys," said Candon.

They followed him to the cabin, where they took their seats, whilst he filled and lit a pipe. Then, with the pipe in his mouth, he sat with his arms resting on the table and his eyes fixed straight before him.

George and the rat trap inventor spoke not a word. They had come to recognise B. C. as the better man in a lot of ways, and they had, unconsciously or sub-consciously, chosen him for their leader in this business that very plainly meant life or death. They were about to attack a hornets' nest, every hornet man-size and armed with a little hatchet instead of a sting. They had no side arms, nothing but the Luggers. On the leader everything would depend and they felt they could depend on Candon.

"We've got an hour and a half before we need stir," suddenly spoke B. C., "and I've got the plan of how to work this business all laid out in my head. Maybe you'll leave it at that for I've taken notice that too much talking muddles things. You're willing to take my word to go when the time comes and follow me?"

"Yes," said Hank.

Candon slipped the old Waltham he wore from its chain and laid it on the table before him.

"That being so," said he, "I want half an hour's talk with you two on something that's got nothing to do with this business. Don't put in any questions or say a word till I get through. For the last three days I've been keeping my head shut against my better feelings, and only for the fact that the whole three of us may be laid out before morning, I'd have gone on, maybe, keeping it shut against my will, so to say, for you are two of the whitest men I've ever fell in with. Boys, I've let you down cruel. I promised you the Dutchman and you shall have him and I promised to lead you to where he'd stowed his takings and that promise holds. All the same, I've not been straight with you. I've got to make things straight, right away or bust, that's how I feel. Well, here's the start. We're after a man by the name of Vanderdecken; that's not his name, the tom-fool newspapers put it on him, but let it hold for a minute while I tell you. This fellow was no Dutchman; American born he was, of decent parents, but born wild and took his hook to sea when he wasn't more'n fourteen. Now seeing we're hunting him I want to give you his character's far as I can get it and show you maybe he's not such a shark as people have made out and was born for something better than the inside of a penitentiary where he's sure going when we have him lugged back to 'Frisco.

"So, I'm telling you, he hadn't been at sea more'n a year when he saved two men's lives from drowning and he hadn't been more'n three years when he got a berth as fourth officer aboard a Cape Horner. After that he rose steady, educating himself in sea practice and land ways, reading everything he could lay his claws on. Maybe it would have been better if he'd kept his eyes shut and worked along blind like most chaps. But he couldn't stop thinking. I reckon thinking ruins more men than drink. The world seemed all upside down to him with the rich bugs a-top same as the fleas on a dog's back."

"So they are," said Hank. "Heave ahead."

"Well," went on the other, "he rose, not having any use for liquor and being a good practical sea-man, till he got his master's ticket and command of a full rigged packet in the Shireman line, then he lost his ship through no fault of his and got fired. The Shiremans had a down on him over stores he'd condemned as not fit for dogs, let alone able seamen, and they'd got wind he was a socialist, and they crabbed him all over the shipping companies' offices. Y'know they're all hand in glove with their secret reports and so on, and Vanderdecken couldn't go into a company's office unless it was to be shown out. Having to eat he went back to the foc'sle—that was in Liverpool, and worked his way to 'Frisco. From there he got to Nome and struck it rich in the Klondyke and got robbed. Then he began to float up and down through more traverses than I've time to tell you of till the Big War came and he heard of the Lusitania. That drove him clean bughouse and he got across the pond and joined up with the British in the submarine fight and got blown up in drifters till he was nearly deaf. Then back he came to 'Frisco, which was his port of choice, and more'n a year ago, he joins up with McGinnis in working the *Heart of Ireland* on all sorts of jobs down the coast, shark fishing, sea scraping and contraband. He was a pretty sick man, was Vanderdecken, with the world and the way it had used him, but it wasn't till prohibition came along that he rose. The hull place went dry and they chucked the liquor down the drains in Santa Barbara, all that wasn't hid away in rich men's cellars. Vanderdecken wasn't a drinking man, but one day at Santa Barbara he saw a lot of money bugs in white ducks popping champagne corks on a yacht and that blew him up. He went to Pat McGinnis and said he, 'Look here, Pat, I've got a notion, let's lay for a yacht and collar their drink and chuck it overboard.' Pat didn't seem to see the use of that, nor how it would bring him profit, but he turned it over in his thick head and the idea came to him of holding a yacht up and robbing it. He worked up the idea and put it before

Vanderdecken who fell in with it like a fool, on the condition that the drink should be hove over. Vanderdecken wasn't after plunder, but he'd gone bughouse on getting even with the champagne guys, and he had to fall in with the other and pretend he was. Then, when everything was fixed up, Pat got cold feet, not from virtue but fright, and nothing would have been done if Vanderdecken hadn't taken hold of the business and gingered the chaps up. He took command of the whole business and then the fun began, and when it began Vanderdecken found himself as keen on taking the valuables as on dousing the drink. But there wasn't much in it. D'you know for all the hullaballoo that's been raised, only three yachts were raided, that's a fact. It was a business that wouldn't bear much repeating and only one haul was really lucky, for the fellow had his wife aboard and all her diamonds and jewels; anyhow, taking it all together, the plunder didn't amount to more'n ten or fifteen thousand dollars leaving the jewels aside, and they might be worth ten thousand. No knowing till they were sold. But there was a lot of fizz and claret sent to hell, but you never heard of that. The yacht owners kept that dark, they didn't want to be laughed at for one thing, and another, the rich folk are mortally afraid of the poor folk suddenly rising and batting them over the head on the drink question, and I've just been thinking, boys, that when Vanderdecken's led back to 'Frisco, there'll be no penitentiary for him lest the rich man's cellar business should be brought too much to notice, and the guys who are poor and dry may say, 'Let's do what Vanderdecken had the guts to do'. However, after the last holdup, the *Heart of Ireland* made for the Bay of Whales and Vanderdecken and McGinnis cached the takings, and Vanderdecken changed the cache unknown to McGinnis. Getting towards 'Frisco, Vanderdecken showed his hand by hinting, like a fool, that the stolen boodle ought to be returned to its owners. That roused McGinnis' hair and the bristles on the hull crowd. They thought they were going to be done. They let Vanderdecken ashore, but a man went with him to watch him and the first thing Vanderdecken heard was that you two were going out in a schooner to hunt for him. He knew he'd never get away from 'Frisco and McGinnis without a knife in his back, so, giving the chap that was with him the slip, he hoofed it for Sullivan's wharf, and dropped aboard the *Wear Jack*. Boys, I'm Vanderdecken!"

CHAPTER XVIII

THE ATTACK

THEY had guessed it for the last few minutes of the yarn. To gauge the effect upon them, one must remember that they were out to hunt the narrator, fearing to be guyed if they did not catch him. What would the guying be like when the real fact was known? The fact that they had been sailing to hunt for Vanderdecken with Vanderdecken on board, and not only on board but acting as sailing master. It was the sort of joke that becomes immortal, like the joke about Handy Andy throwing the wash jug out of the window instead of the water, the sort of story that would preserve the protagonists in ridicule, not for years but for ages.

And yet there was no spark of anger in the mind of Hank, or in the mind of George. Candon, by his confession and story and evident regret for the business, had drawn their teeth; also in the last few days he had taught them to like and admire him, and in some extraordinary way he had in the last few minutes made them feel that their affairs were subordinate to his and that they were only side characters in a story that was his.

All the same in the mind of each lay the fact that they had been done brown and the conviction that B. C. must now never be taken by the police even if they had to shoot him.

Hank was the first to speak.

"Well," said he, "it's a Kid Lewis of a punch, there's no denying it, and if it was all from your own shoulder, B. C., I'm not saying I wouldn't have hit back, but there's more in this than a man can see. Maybe I'm talking through my hat, but seems to me it's curious. Me putting out on this show and J. B. advertising me and you coming into 'Frisco on top of the advertisement and taking it up. Well, there's no use in talking, let's clean the slate. I'm not sure if an expedition was putting out to collar Hank Fisher, I wouldn't join it same as you did, specially if I had the McGinnis crowd after me. What do you say, Bud?"

"Oh," said George, "what's the good of talking. Forget it."

"That's easy said," put in Candon, "mind you, I don't blame myself for joining in with you same as I did, you were after me, anyhow, and I didn't know you from Adam, but it was a low-down trick making you sign that contract, binding you to put me ashore with five thousand dollars in my pocket after handing you over the Dutchman, which was myself. That's what's been getting me the last few days. It was just the same with the yacht business. I started out only to douse the liquor, but when it came to stripping the diamonds and money off those ducks I was as keen as McGinnis, then when the thing was done and the stuff safely hived, I was mortal sorry for myself. I've got a black streak in me and that's the truth, nigger black, and there's no use talking."

"No matter," said Hank. "Forget it. You've got a damn big white streak in you, B. C. I reckon we're all pretty much striped if it comes to that—anyhow what we've got to do now is save that girl and get the boodle. You can skip when we've collared the stuff—it'll be something to bring back to 'Frisco anyhow."

"I'm going back with you to 'Frisco," said Candon, "I'm not afraid to face the music."

"Well, there's time enough to talk about that," put in the other. "The thing is now to get the girl. Time's up and we've got to start. What's your plan?"

"Rush them," said Candon. "Three of our Chinks will be enough with us to help in the shouting, go and pick three of them, will you? Then we'll row ashore, leave the boat beached, crawl over those rocks 'tween us and the next bay, get right up to the edge of their camp and stampede them, shouting like ballyhoos and firing over their heads. One of us had better look after the girl and pick her up and waltz off with her, I reckon I'm the strongest, maybe, and I'll do the snatching—don't use more than two rounds apiece when you let off over their heads, you'll maybe want the rest if the hatchet men show fight."

"That's clear," said Hank. "I'll go pick the Chinks."

He left the cabin and the two others turned their attention to the Lugger pistols, emptied the magazines, oiled them, tried the mechanism and refilled them. Then with the pistols and extra ammunition they came on deck.

The waning moon had not yet risen, but the stars were beginning to blaze, and against them the peak of San Nicolas with its cloud top looked like a giant with a turbaned head. Through the windless night the wash of the waves on the beach came clear, rhythmical, slumbrous like the pulse of the sleeping sea.

Hank had got his men into the boat, he took the pistol handed to him by Candon and the ammunition, then, with a glance at the deck where Charley was in charge, he led the way overside and the boat pushed off.

"You're sure of the Chinks?" asked George in a whisper as they rowed.

"Sure," replied Hank. "I've told them they've only got to shout and I'll give five dollars to the chap that shouts the loudest. I tipped them that these guys have got an American girl with them and that the American Government will plaster them with dollars if we get her away—Oh, they're right enough. Now, not a word out of you all when we get to the beach. Just follow B. C. and hold your breath for the shouting."

The boat grounded on the soft sand and they tumbled out, hauled her up a few feet and Hank, taking a small lantern he had brought with him, lit it and placed it on the sands close to the bow. Then they started. Europe in the van, Asia in the rear.

The rocks were soon reached. The rocks just here are easy to negotiate, great flat-topped masses rising gradually from the bayside to a summit that falls as gradually to the sands of the bay beyond.

When they reached the summit the blaze of two fires on the beach showed out close together, their light blending in an elliptical zone, beyond which the tents hinted of themselves.

"The Chinks are round one, the white men by the other," said Candon. "Couldn't be better for we've got them divided. Now then, you two, follow me and do as I do—and for the love of Mike don't sneeze. Got your guns handy? That's right."

He began the descent. Then when they reached the sands he got on hands and knees.

Scarcely had he done so than the notes of a guitar came through the night from the camp of the white slavers and the first words of a song. They could not make out the words, but they could tell at once that the singer was neither American nor English. That high nasal voice spoke of Spain where the cicadas shrill in the plane trees in the heat-shaken air.

"Dagoes," said Hank.

"Come on," said Candon.

Then, had anyone been watching, across the sands towards the zone of firelight, six forms might have been seen crawling, liker to land crabs than the forms of men or beasts.

The Chinks around their fire were broken up into parties playing games and smoking. By the white man's fire sat the guitar player on a camp stool, the light full on his sharp profile, another man leaning on his elbow lay smoking cigarettes, and a woman seated on the sand, an elderly-looking woman of Jewish type, was engaged in some sort of needlework, and her hand as it moved, seemed covered with rings.

George thought he had never beheld a more sinister looking trio. The girl was nowhere to be seen.

George, Hank and Candon put their heads together.

"She's in one of the tents," whispered B. C., "tied up for the night most like."

"Shall we rush them now?" asked Hank.

"Yep, get your guns ready. Look! There's the girl! Now then, boys!"

The girl who had just left the most seaward of the tents stood for a moment with the vague light of the fire touching her. She was very small. To George, in that half moment, she seemed only a child, and the sight of her contrasted with her captors came to them as though timed to the moment.

The beach blazed out with noise, the ear-splitting explosions of the Luggers and the yells of the attackers swept the man on the sands to his feet. George saw, as one sees in a dream, the whole of the Chinese casting cards and dice and flying like leaves driven by the broom of the wind. He had a vision of Hank downing the cigarette smoker, then he got a smash on the head from a guitar and was rolling on the sands with a man who was shouting "Hell, hell, hell!" punching him to silence whilst the woman with nails in his neck was trying to strangle him, screaming all the time till Hank dragged her off, crying, "We've got the girl—come on—come on! We've got the girl!" Then the nightmare shifted and he was running, Candon in front of him with something on his shoulder that struggled and fought and screamed for help, then he was stumbling over rocks, Hank helping him, Hank laughing and whooping like a man in delirium, and shouting to the stars: "We've got the girl! We've got the girl!"

Then came the glow-worm glimmer of the lamp by the boat, and the boat with them all crowding into it, Chinks and all, and the musky smell of the Chinks, the push off and a great silence broken only by the oars and Candon's voice crying, "Lord! she's dead!" and Hank's voice, "No, she ain't, only fainted."

The *Wear Jack's* side with Charley showing a lantern, the getting on board with their helpless bundle, and the vanishing of Candon with her down the companion way to the saloon, then and only then did things shake back to reality whilst Hank took both George's hands in his. "Bo, we've done it," said Hank.

"We sure have," said George.

Which was a fact—if they only had known.

CHAPTER XIX

A SEA FIGHT

MEANWHILE the Chinks with absolute imperturbability and under the orders of Charley, were getting the boat on board. As it came on deck Candon appeared.

"She's come to," said Candon. "I've stuck her in the bunk in the after cabin, but she's so rattled she won't speak—just lays there. Hurry up with the anchor, you boys. Listen!"

From shoreward through the night came sounds, far-away shouting and then the throb of a gong.

"Those guys are collecting the hatchet men," cried Hank, "they'll maybe try and cut us off from the next bay—there was a boat on the sands. Lord! and I've dropped my Lugger."

"I've got mine," said George.

"Mine's in the cabin," said Candon, "get the windlass going and I'll start the engine. Give me a call when the mud hook's up and look slippy." He dived below and as he dived a loose bunt of sail puffed out and a breeze from the nor'west laid its fingers on the cheek of Hank.

"Wind's coming," cried Hank. "Leave the windlass, get to the halyards. Hi! Charley there, look alive, man. Your throat and peak halyards—Bud, lay forward and get the gaskets off the jib." He rushed to the hatch of the engine room. "Candon, below there! Wind's coming, I'm getting sail on her, that damned junk will lay for us sure and I'm not trusting the engine any." He rushed back to the wheel and stood whilst the mainsail, fore and jib were got on her. Then came the sound of the winch and the anchor came home whilst the slatting canvas filled and Hank turned the spokes of the wheel setting her on a course south by east.

Candon's head bobbed up from below.

"I can't get the durned thing to go," said he.

"Never mind," said Hank, "the wind's freshening."

As he spoke it breezed up strong, the mainsheet tautened and the boom lifted as the sails bellied hard against the stars and the *Wear Jack* leaned over to it, boosting the ebony water to snow.

Candon took the wheel from Hank.

"It's bad luck we have to run right past them," said he as the next bay opened, showing the junk lit up as if for a festival and the fires on the beach.

"They'll have had time to collect their wits and man the junk and they'll know it's not the police."

"Oh, we've got the heels of them," said Hank.

"Hope so," said the other. "Look! they're getting sail on her."

In the dim light the vast lug sail of the junk could be seen rising and even before it fully took the wind, she was moving.

"They're rowing!" cried George. "Look! they've got the sweeps out!"

Candon looked. The fag end of a moon rising over the hills of California showed now clearly the junk putting out to sea ahead of them, the flash and movement of the sweeps, the great lubberly lateen sail being trimmed and the foam dashing from the bow.

"They've got us," said Hank, "get your guns ready if it comes to boarding. Where's yours, B. C.?" "Down in the cabin?—one sec." He dived below. Then he came up again. "Cabin door's bolted."

"Whach you say?" cried Candon.

"Cabin door's bolted, can't get in—"

"Maybe it's stuck," said Candon. "Don't bother with it, we've no time for fiddling, lay hold of something to bat these chaps with if they try and board. Hell! but she's racing,—that junk."

She was. Urged by wind and oars, making ahead to hit the course of the *Wear Jack* at an acute angle, she seemed bound to do it.

"What's her game?" asked George.

"Foul us, get broadside on and board us," replied Candon.

"How'd it be to put her about and get her on a wind?" asked Hank.

"No use, going about would give her lengths—those junks shoot up into the wind like all possessed and the sweeps help—Leave her to me."

The *Wear Jack* kept on.

Racing now almost parallel—the junk ahead with sweeps drawn in, the two boats held only half a cable length apart. They could see the junk's deck swarming, the hatchet men, now that they had got their courage were voicing it, and yells like the strident sound of tearing calico came mixed with the wash of the waves and the beating of a gong. Closer they got, still closer, the *Wear Jack* gaining under a strengthening flaw of the wind. Then, with a shout and with a lightning movement, Candon, to the horror of the others, put his helm hard over. The *Wear Jack* checked, shied just like a horse, and with a thunder of slatting canvas, and rattling blocks, plunged at the junk, ramming her abaft the chunky mast. The fellow at the steering sweep shifted his helm to get clear, the junk forged to starboard and the bowsprit of the *Wear Jack*, like a clutching hand, snapped stay after stay bringing the great sail down like a Venetian blind over the crowd on deck.

"We're free," shouted Candon, "bowsprit's half gone. No matter, get forward, Hank, and clear the raffle!"

Then as the *Wear Jack* forged ahead, the Kiro Shiwo drifting her faster than the junk, the wind took her sails.

"They aren't sinking, are they?" cried George.

"Sinking—nothing," replied B. C., turning his head. "They'll get back ashore with their sweeps. If they were, it'd be a good job. What's the damage, Hank?"

"Bob stay gone," came Hank's voice. "Bowsprit seems all right—Lord, it's a miracle."

Then he came aft having set Charley and the Chinks on repairs.

"B. C.," said Hank, "you're a marvel. What put it into your nut to do it?"

"It came to me," said the other, "they'd have done it to us in another tick, got fast and downed us. Hit first—that's my motto."

"Well," said Hank, "you've done it."

Away back in the moonlight across the heave of the sea, they could make out the dismasted wreck floundering like a drunken thing, listing to starboard with the weight of her broken wing, *gastados*, out of the running—done for.

CHAPTER XX

DOWN BELOW

GEORGE and Hank went forward to superintend the work of the Chinks on the bowsprit; Candon, at the wheel and well content with the work of the night, felt thirsty. There was no one to fetch him a drink, tea was what he fancied and thinking of tea made him think of the tea things which were in the cabin. Then he remembered what Hank had said about the cabin door being closed.

It occurred to him now that the girl had bolted the door. No doubt the poor creature was half crazy with fright. It had not occurred before to the ingenuous and benevolent B. C. that the girl must look on her new captors as more terrible than even the white slavers. The yelling and the shooting, the stampeding of the camp, the way she had been seized, caught up and carried off—why, what must she think of them! Up to this he had been too busy to think himself. It was only now, as Hank would have said, that the thing suddenly hit him on the head like an orange.

"Hank!" shouted B. C.

"Coming," replied Hank. He came aft.

"I'm thinking of the girl down below, it's she that's most likely fastened the door, she's most likely scared out of her life the way we've took her off and not knowing who we are."

"Sure," said Hank.

"She nearly tore my head off as I was carrying her—I remember getting a cat out of a trap once, it acted just the same—scared—"

"Listen," said Hank, who was standing close to the cabin skylight.

The skylight was a bit open and fastened from inside; through the opening came sounds as of someone moving about.

"She's moving," said B. C. "She's got over her fright. Down with you, Hank, and get her story, tell her I'll be down when George comes aft, tell her she's as safe with us as she'd be with her gran'mother."

Hank descended.

Candon heard him knock—then his voice.

"Halloo there."

Silence.

"Halloo there."

Then came a determined little voice.

"Clear off—I've got a pistol—"

Candon, listening, remembered the Lugger pistol he had left on the cabin table.

Then Hank's voice.

"Don't be scared, com'n' open the door, don't be scared."

The voice: "I'm not a person to be scared—you ought to know that."

Down below the perplexed Hank, standing before the closed door, was at pause for a moment. Why ought he to have known that? Was she mad after all?

"Well, open the door anyhow," said he. "Don't you know we're your friends. Good Lord, don't you know what we've risked getting you away from that lot? Come on—all the food and stuff's in the lockers and lazarette and we're clean perishing for something to eat."

"That's good," said the voice, "you'll have to perish till morning, then we'll talk. Now go away, please."

"Whach you say?"

"Scatter."

A long pause. Then Hank's voice, angry. "I tell you what—I wish to the Lord we'd left you there."

And the voice: "You'll be wishing it more when you're in the penitentiary."

Then Candon could almost hear the perplexed Hank scratching his head. A long pause. Then Hank:

"But for the Lord's sake, you don't think we want to do you any harm?"

The voice: "Then what did you want to do?"

Hank: "Get you away from that lot."

The voice: "What for?"

Hank: "What *for*—why to save you from them—to save you body and soul—didn't you *know* they were taking you to perdition,—clean perdition."

Then the voice, after a moment's pause: "I don't know whether you're toughs or religious cranks. It doesn't matter. Anyhow this door doesn't open s'long as it's dark. Now clear, come again in the morning and, if you take my advice, steer straight for Santa Barbara. If you put me ashore safe by morning maybe I'll try and help you with the police, but I don't promise—now clear."

Hank cleared.

On deck he found George who had come aft. "She's gone bughouse," said Hank, "or else she was one of them, helping in the contraband."

He recounted the dialogue. "She's got that Lugger pistol and seems to me, boys, she's got the game. It's worse than Pittsburg. Called me a religious crank. Anyhow she's got us, got the grub under her thumb unless we make out with the rice and truck the Chinks feed on."

"I can't make it out," said George. "I'd have sworn by the look we got at her, through the glass, that she was a prisoner with those scamps. D'y' remember the way she carried on, went and threw herself down on the ground with her face hidden in her arm?"

"Seems to me," said Hank, "we've been reading into the situation more than was in it. She was no prisoner. She was one of them—daughter most likely of that Jew woman I hauled off you—well, I wish we'd left her alone—and to think of the size of her sitting up and crowing like that."

"Oh, it's nothing," said George, "it's the day of the flapper. She most likely was running that show. It's part of the new world—the millennium that was to come after the war!"

Candon alone said nothing. The thing had hit him even harder than Hank. The knight errant in him was flattened out, at least for the moment. He remembered the cat he had released from the trap and how it had clawed him—but it had taken milk from his hand immediately after and become his friend, whereas this creature—! Then it came to him out of his own mind—for Hank's words had produced little effect on him—that the truth was he had released her from no trap. She was part and parcel with those scoundrels, a vicious girl made vicious no doubt from bad association. This conviction suddenly coming to his mind produced an uplift.

"Boys," said B. C. suddenly, "we'll tame her. There's something moving in this more than we can see. Anyhow, we've got her away from those ginks to start with."

"That's true," said Hank, his mind taking suddenly the colour of Candon's. But George was of rougher stuff than these idealists. He went to the skylight and cautiously tried to peep, but could see nothing, then he listened but could hear nothing. He came back to the others.

"She's lying down, most likely, can't see her or hear her—it's all very well talking of taming—what do you think this show is? I didn't start out to tame girls, don't know how to begin, either,—I know, it's as much my fault as yours—we shouldn't have mixed up in the business—and I tell you we are in a tight place. That crowd will swear anything against us and she'll back them. She talked of the police. That's just so, all these white slavers and dope sellers and contrabanders are hand in glove with the police. They couldn't do their business else; we should have left them alone."

"Now that's clean wrong," said Hank. "Doesn't matter a rap if the girl's a tough, we saved her, anyhow. We did the right thing and she can't make it wrong by being wrong herself."

"That's a fact," said Candon.

"Maybe," replied George. "All the same she's done us out of our bunks, and what are you going to do with her, anyway? Here you are tied up with a girl, you've taken her from her mother, if that old Jew woman was her mother, ripped her clean out of her environment, she's on our hands. If she doesn't go back to that lot, what are we to do with her?"

Hank got peppery. "Why in the nation didn't you think of that before we took her," asked he.

"Why you know well enough," answered the other, "we thought that lot had stolen her away from her people, naturally I thought we'd put her back again with her people, whereas, now, look where we are. Suppose even we do tame her, as you call it, and she goes straight, who's to feed her and keep her?"

"Why, Bud," said Hank, "we'll manage somehow. Look at you with all your dollars, what better use could you make of a few of them, and we'll help."

"Yes, we'll help," said Candon, forgetting the fact that he was due for either the penitentiary or hoofing it to Callao from the Bay of Whales. "We'll help and the three of us will make out somehow."

The millionaire said nothing for a moment. He was about to fly out at the cool way these benefactors of humanity were disposing of his credit and coin. Then he calmed down and said nothing and went forward to get some of the "rice and truck the Chinks feed on" for his companions, also a beaker of water.

The weather was warm, so warm that sleeping on deck was no penance and Charley being called to the wheel the *Wear Jack* and her strange cargo snored on south—ever south—under the night of stars.

CHAPTER XXI

TOMMIE

HANK and Candon were asleep, whilst George stood as officer of the watch. A great blaze of light fanning up beyond the coast hills showed the *Wear Jack* under all plain sail and the gulls following her, royal terns and loons and black-headed gulls, whilst far above a Brandt's cormorant formed an escort in the blue, wheeling, dropping as though to pierce the deck, and then passing off with a cry, northward, towards the vanished islands.

Away over there to the east, fog held the lower hills and made a country of rolling snow to the sea edge, a country now white, now golden as the great sun rose above it, now breaking here and there, and now flying before the wind like the banners of a shattered army.

At eight o'clock, when they had breakfasted somehow out of materials supplied by Charley, Hank suddenly took the wheel of affairs.

Not a sound had broken the ominous silence down below and up to now the barred-out men had not spoken a word on the matter.

"It's lucky for us we have a crew of Chinks," said Hank suddenly and apropos of nothing, "the Chinks don't know and if they did they wouldn't care. If we took our breakfast standing on our heads it would be all the same to them. Well, see here, you fellows, what we going to do? We have to get done with this business right now. I've got a stiff back sleeping in the scuppers and I don't propose to feed for the rest of my natural on this Chow junk. Seeing I did the talking last night, I propose going down to prospect and have a parley."

"Right!" said the other two with a sudden brightening, as though a burden had been lifted from them.

"If she won't open," said Hank, as he got on his long legs, "I'll bust that door in. You keep your ears skinned at the hatch and come along down if there's trouble."

They moved up close to the hatch and Hank went down. They heard his knock and almost immediately on the knock a clear voice say: "Yes?"

Then Hank: "It's come day now, will you open? I want to have a word with you."

The voice: "Yes. I will open, on one condition, that after I have drawn the bolts you will wait till I give the word before you come in."

"Right."

"If you don't, I'll shoot."

"Right."

They heard the bolts being drawn. Then, after a moment, giving her time to get to the other end of the cabin, they heard her cry, "Come in."

Then her voice: "Well?"

Silence.

The voice: "Well—what on earth is the matter with you? Can't you speak?"

Hank: "I'm clean knocked out. Suffering Moses!"

The voice: "I don't want to know anything about Moses and his sufferings, I just want to know who you are, the name of this ship, and what you mean. Don't come nearer!"

Hank: "I'm not—Can't you see I'm hit? This has been a mistake."

The voice: "I should think so."

Hank: "Now I see you in the light of day, the whole thing has jumped together in my head—Lord! what a mistake."

The voice: "Well?"

Hank: "I'll get on deck for a moment if you don't mind. I'm hit."

The voice: "So you have said. Well, get on deck and recover yourself and be quick about it—if it's a mistake you've got to mend it and get me back—go on."

Hank came on deck, he beckoned to the others and led them forward.

"Boys."

"Go *on*!"

"Boys, it's Tommie Coulthurst."

The awful silence that followed this crushing announcement lasted for full twenty seconds, a silence broken only by the slash of the bow wash, the creak of a block and the cry of the gulls.

Then George said: "Oh, Lord!"

"You ain't mistaken?" asked Candon feebly. Hank did not even reply.

"But we've busted their ship," said George, as if protesting against the enormity of the idea that had just put itself together in his brain, "and I nearly did for that gink with the guitar."

"I know," said Hank, "and I downed that other chap and hauled that Jew woman off you by the left leg—well, there we are. "What's wrong with this cruise anyhow?"

"I dunno," said George. "My head's turned inside out. Down with you, Hank, and get her up—get her up, we've gotta try and explain. Down with you."

Hank started aft on a run and vanished. A minute later a deck chair appeared at the hatch, followed by Hank. After Hank came a little hand holding a Lugger pistol, and then the head and body of Tommie Coulthurst.

She looked smaller even than by the firelight, small but so exquisitely proportioned that you did not bother about her size. She had no hat, her steadfast seaweed brown eyes were fixed on the men before her and the strange and extraordinary thing was that her face as she gazed at them brought them comfort of a kind.

For Tommie's face, though small enough, had nothing small in it. It was good to look upon as Truth and Honesty and Courage could make it and Beauty had lent a hand.

Hank put out the chair.

"Will you sit down," said Hank.

Before sitting down she took a glance round at the deck and the Chink at the wheel. Then as though the pistol were bothering her, she threw it into the scupper. She seemed to have read everything in the situation and found no danger.

"Well," said she, "what on earth is it all?"

"It's a mistake," said Hank.

"So you have told me—but seems to me we are getting further from Santa Barbara, we are going down the coast, aren't we?"

"We are," said George, "and I'll put the ship about right away if you like—only I'd ask you to listen to us first and a few miles more or less don't matter."

"Go on," said Tommie.

George, who had recovered his wits sooner than the others, had seized on an idea. Maybe it was Tommie's face that inspired it.

"The whole of this business is a most awful mix-up," he began. "First I'd better tell you who we are. My name's Du Cane. George Harley du Cane. This is Mr. Hank Fisher, and this is Mr. Candon. I don't know if you have read in the papers of a yacht putting out from San Francisco to catch Vanderdecken, the man who has been raiding yachts?"

"Yes," said Tommie, "I know about it."

"Well, this is the yacht. We got along down to San Nicolas and going ashore we saw a Chinese camp. We spotted you through a glass and came to the conclusion you were in the hands of Chinese white slavers. We made up our minds to rescue you."

"Good Lord!" said Tommie, sitting forward in her chair with wide pupils.

"And seems to me we did it," said George. "Can you imagine anything more horrible?"

Tommie's mouth was open, relaxed, yet in a way rigid. She seemed in the grip of petrified laughter.

"Not only that," went on George, "but we knocked the mast out of that junk. She chased us and we rammed her. What was she? Part of your show?"

Tommie's mouth had suddenly closed itself, laughter had vanished and her eyes shone.

"Yes, part of our show."

"And those were real Chinks—hatchet men?"

"Yep—we always work with real stuff."

"We ought to have recognized you," went on George, "we've seen you often enough in the pictures and the press, but the distance was too big, besides looking from a distance you gave us the impression—we saw you throw yourself down."

"I was showing Mr. Althusen a pose," said Tommie.

"Althusen?"

"The producer."

"Was that the man playing the guitar by the fire?"

"Yep." Her eyes still blazed strangely. Hank thought she was going to fly out at them.

"He smashed his guitar on me," said George. "It's awful."

"I think it's *splendid*!" said Tommie.

CHAPTER XXII

A PROBLEM IN PSYCHOLOGY

IF the deck had opened delivering up Mr. Althusen and his broken guitar the three men could not have been more astonished.

"I think it's splendid," she said again. "You saw everything all wrong, but how could you know. I think it's just fine. Those hatchet men were a tough crowd and they'd have killed you for sure only you scattered them like you did. You saw a girl being kidnapped as you thought and you just dashed in. Nobody but white Americans would have acted like that."

"Oh, anyone would," murmured Hank.

"No they wouldn't—they'd gone off for the police or said, 'Oh, my, how shocking,' and gone off about their business. You struck. Well, I'm sorry for locking you out, but I'm like yourselves, I didn't know."

"Oh, that's nothing," said George.

Tommie's eyes were fixed on Candon.

"It was you collared me," said she to him.

The blue eyes of Candon met the liquid brown eyes of Tommie.

He nodded his head.

Tommie considered him for a moment attentively, as though he were an object of curiosity or a view—anything but a living male being. It was sometimes a most disconcerting thing about her, this detachment from all trammels of sex and convention, the detachment of a child. She seemed making up her mind whether she liked him or not and doing it quite openly, and her mind seemed still not quite made up when, with a sigh, she came to.

"Well," said she, "and now about getting back."

"That's the question now," said George hurriedly and with his lips suddenly gone dry so that he had to moisten them. "We've got to get you back."

"Yes, that's so," said Hank, unenthusiastically. "We've got to do it somehow or 'nother."

"Look here," said George, suddenly taking his courage in both hands. "I don't mind the row we're sure to get into, it's the guying that gets me. Think of the papers. When we started out on this fool business we got it pretty hot—and now this on top of everything."

"I know," said Tommie. She was sitting forward in her chair, clasping her knees, biting her lip in thought and staring at the deck planking. She saw the position of the unfortunates as clearly as they did. The fact that these men had done for her a fine and chivalrous action which was still absurd hit her in an extraordinary way. Her sturdy and honest little soul revolted at the thought of what the press would make of the business. She could hear the laughter only waiting to be touched off, she could read the scare head-lines. She knew, for publicity was part of her life.

The stage was already prepared for the farce: by now every paper in America would be setting up the story of how Tommie Coulthurst had been abducted. It only waited for these men to be dragged on as the abductors amidst a roar of laughter that would sound right round the world.

She had read in the Los Angeles papers the humorous comments on them and their expedition and now, this!

No, it must not be.

For a moment she looked back at the scene of the night before, finer than any scene in a cinema play, real, dramatic, heroic, yet seemingly based on absurdity—was it absurdity? Not a bit—not unless the finer promptings of humanity were absurd and courage and daring ridiculous. They had risked a lot, these men, and she had never in her life before seen men in action. Ridicule of them would hit every fibre of her being. No, it must not be. Question was how to save them.

"Say," said Tommie, suddenly clasping her knees tighter and looking up, "we're in a tough tangle, aren't we?"

The others seemed to agree. "Sam Brown," went on Tommie, "he's one of the electric men at the Wallack Studios, caught a rat an' put it in a flower pot with a slate on top and a weight on the slate and left it till next morning; he keeps dogs, an' came to find it and it was gone, said it must have got out and put the slate back, and Wallack told us to remember that rat if we were ever cornered by difficulties in our work an' take as our motto, 'Never say die till you're dead.' Well, we're in a tight place but we aren't dead. Question is what's the first thing to do?"

"The first thing," said Hank, "why, it's to get you back safe."

"I'm safe enough," said Tommie. "It's not a question of safety s'much as smothering this thing. S'pose we put back now to Santa Barbara, where'd you be? No, the first thing is to get you time. I reckon that rat would have been eaten if he hadn't had time to think his way out or if someone hadn't foozled along and loosed him. What's your plans? You said you were out after Vanderdecken, where'd you expect to catch him?"

Hank looked at Candon and noticed that he had turned away.

"Well, it's not him we are after now so much as his boodle," said Hank. "We know where it's hid and we want to get it."

"Where's it hid?"

"Place called the Bay of Whales down below Cape St. Lucas."

"How long will it take you to fetch there and back?"

"About a fortnight, maybe."

Tommie considered for a moment.

"Well," she said at last, "seems to me that the only thing to do is to go on till we meet some ship that'll take me back. When I get back I'll have to do a lot of lying, that's all. Ten to one they'll put this business down to Vanderdecken and maybe I'll say Vanderdecken took me and you collared me back from him—how'd that be?"

Candon turned. He struck his right fist into his open left palm. "There's more'n this than I can get the lie of," said B. C. as if to himself.

"What you say?" asked Tommie.

"Oh, he means it's a mix-up," said George. "But see here—we can't do it."

"Which?"

"We can't put more on you than we've done already. I know, I was mean enough to want you to go on with us when I started that talk about our being guyed—it's different now."

"Yep," said Hank.

"Sure," said Candon.

"Have you done?" asked Tommie. "Well then I'm going on, where's the damage? I'm used to the rough and the open. That film we were working on is finished and I guess a few days' holiday won't do me any harm. B'sides it works up the publicity. Why, every day I'm away is worth a thousand dollars to Wallacks, leaving myself alone. They'll book that film in Timbuctoo. Do you see? It's no trouble to me, why should you worry? Now I propose we get something to eat."

"But how about clothes," asked George.

"Which, mine? Oh, I reckon I'll manage somehow. The thing that gets me is a toothbrush."

"Thank God," said George.

"Which?"

"I've got four new ones," said the millionaire.

CHAPTER XXIII

THE NEW CHUM

THE extraordinary thing about Miss Coulthurst was the absence and yet the presence of the feminine in her. Possessed of all the electrical properties of a woman and the chummable properties of a man, this dangerous individual presiding at the breakfast table of the *Wear Jack* and dispensing tea to her captors created an atmosphere in which even the fried eggs seemed part of romantic adventure.

The sordid had dropped out of everything, fear of consequences had vanished for the moment, the shifting sunlight on the Venesta panelings, the glitter of the Tyrebuck tea things, the warm sea-scented air blowing through the skylight,—everything bright and pleasant seemed to the hypnotised ones part of Tommie.

There was no making conversation at that breakfast party. Shut up all night with no one to talk to, she did the talking, explaining first of all and staging for their consideration the people they had attacked the night before. Althusen was the biggest producer in Los Angeles—that is to say the world, and Moscovitch, the camera man, was on all fours with him, Mrs. Raphael was Julia Raphael, the actress, and the play was "The Chink and the Girl." The hatchet men were real *kai-gingh* and Tommie was the girl they were making off with, and the scene on San Nicolas was not the end of the play but somewhere in the middle, for pictures are produced in sections labelled and numbered and sometimes the end sections are produced first.

Tommie had been born on a ranch. She was quite free with her private history. Her father was Ben Coulthurst—maybe they'd heard of him. Well, anyway, he was well-known in Texas till he went broke and died and left Tommie to the care of an aunt who lived in San Francisco where Tommie was half smothered—she couldn't stand cities—and maybe would have died if the movie business hadn't come along and saved her. Fresh air stunts, as they knew, were her vocation, and she guessed she was made of india rubber, seeing up to this she had only broken one collarbone. Her last experience was dropping from an aëroplane on to the top of a sixty-mile-an-hour express.

"I've seen you do that," said Hank. "Made me sweat in the palms of my hands."

Well, that was nothing; plane and express moving at the same speed it was as simple as stepping off the sidewalk; being thrown out of a window was a lot worse. She thanked her Maker she was born so small, but what got her goat was the nicknames her diminutive size had evoked. Some smartie on a Los Angeles paper had called her the "Pocket Artemis." What was an Artemis anyway?

"Search me," said Hank.

"It's a goddess," said George, "same thing as Diana."

Well, she had made him apologise, anyhow.

Candon alone took little part in the conversation. This gentleman, so ready in an emergency, seemed all abroad before the creature he had captured and carried off. He sat absorbing her without neglecting his food and later on when she was on deck he appeared with half an armful of books.

She was a book worm in private life and had hinted at the fact, out of which B. C. made profit.

"Here's some books," said he. "They aren't much, but they're all we've got. That chair comfortable?"

Then they fell into talk, Candon taking his seat beside her on the deck and close to the little heap of books.

They had scarcely spoken to one another at the breakfast table and now, all of a sudden, they were chattering together like magpies. Hank and George, smoking in the cabin down below, could hear their voices through the skylight.

"Wonder what she'd say if she knew," said Hank in a grumbling tone.

"Knew what?" asked George.

"'Bout B. C. being Vanderdecken."

"Oh, she'd ten to one like him all the better," said George. "It's his watch and I wish he'd quit fooling and look after the ship."

"The ship's all right," said Hank.

"What do you mean?"

"You couldn't hurt her or break her on a rock, not till she's done with us; you couldn't rip the masts out of her or put her ashore, not till she's finished with us; she's a mug trap and we're the mugs. I believe Jake put a spell on her. What's to be the end of it? I tell you it makes me crawl down the back when I think of that junk. What made that blue-eyed squatteroo of a B. C. ram her like that for?"

"Well, if he hadn't, she'd have boarded us."

"Boarded us, be hanged! If he'd blame well stuck ashore at 'Frisco, we wouldn't have landed at San Nicolas."

"Well, there's no use whining," said George. "We're in the soup—question is how to get out. We've got to collar that boodle first so's to have something to show."

"Something to show—Lord! We'll be shows enough."

"Well, strikes me since we went into such a damn-fool business—"

Hank snorted. "Well, I didn't pull you in, you would butt in—it's none of my fault."

"Who said it was?"

"I'm not saying who said it was or who said it wasn't—thing is, there's no use in complaining."

"I said that a moment ago."

"Oh, well, there you are—I'm going on deck."

Almost a quarrel and all because the pocket Artemis was chatting to another man who had blue eyes—a blue-eyed squatteroo who was only yesterday good old B. C.

CHAPTER XXIV

THE FREIGHTER

THE sea grew bluer.

Day by day the Kiro Shiwo increased its splendour as the *Wear Jack*, at a steady ten knot clip, left the latitude of Guadeloupe behind, raising Eugenio Point and the heat-hazy coast that stretches to Cape San Pablo.

The threatened difference between Hank and George had died out. The reason of this release was not far to seek. Tommie, at that moment of her life, was as destitute of all the infernal sex wiles of womanhood as a melon. She had no idea of men as anything else than companions; that was why the pocket Artemis failed a bit in love scenes. A year ago she had signed a contract with the Wallack and Jackson Company by which she received forty thousand dollars a year for five years, and Wallack had reason sometimes to grumble. Tommie had no idea of how to fling herself into the arms of movie heroes, or to do the face-work in a close-up when the heroine is exhibiting to the audience the grin and glad eye, or the "Abandon," or the "Passionate Appeal" so dear to the movie fan.

"Good God, that ain't the way to make love," would cry Scudder, her first producer. "Nuzzle him—stop. Now then, make ready and get abandon into it. He's not the plumber come to mend the bath, nor your long-lost brother you wished had remained in 'Urope and you're hugging for the sake of appearance. He's the guy you're in love with. Now then, put some heart, punch and pep into it—now then! Camera!"

No good.

"Oh Lord, oh Lord!" the perspiring Scudder would cry, "looks as if you were nursing a teddy bear. *Strain* him to your heart. Stop flapping your hands on his back. Now, look up in his face—so—astonished yet almost fearful. Can't you understand the wonder of love just born in the human heart, the soul's awakening? Lord! you're not lookin' at an eclipse of the sun! That's better, hang on so, count ten and then nuzzle him."

But despite all directions Tommie was somewhat a failure in passion.

Wallack summed the position up when he declared that it would be worth paying ten thousand dollars a year to some man that would do the soul's awakening business with Tommie. She could laugh, weep, fly into a temper, ride a mustang bare-backed, drive a motor car over a precipice, be as funny in her diminutive way as Charlie Chaplin, but she couldn't make love worth a cent.

That was what Hank Fisher & Co. sensed, when the girl illusion vanished, disclosing a jolly companion and nothing more; sensed, without in the least sensing the fact that owing maybe to her small size, she had a power almost as strong as the power that wakens the wonder of love in the human heart.

Life was different on board, owing to this new importation; busier too. This was an entirely new stunt, to Tommie, and just as she knew everything about an automobile, an aëroplane, and a horse, she seemed determined to know everything about the *Wear Jack*. Her capacity for assimilating detail was phenomenal; the use of everything from the main sheet buffer to the mast winch had to be explained, she had to learn how to steer, and, having learned, she insisted on taking her trick at the wheel. When she was not sitting with her nose in a book, she was helping or hindering in the running of the ship. Then there was the question of her clothes to keep them busy.

Drawing on to the tropics, it was more a question of shedding clothes, especially when it came to the matter of tweed coats and skirts. Bud, in his millionaire way, had come well provided; boxes and boxes had arrived from Hewson & Loder's and had been received by Hank and stowed as "more of Bud's truck." White silk shirts, suits of white drill, they all rose up like a white cloud in George's mind one blue and burning morning as he contemplated Tommie in her stuffy tweeds.

"Look here, T. C.," said George, "you can't get along in that toggery. I've half a dozen suits of white down below and I'll get one of the Chinks to tailor a couple of them for you. Hank, roust out those boxes, will you?"

They tried a white drill coat on her.

They had never really recognised her size till they saw her in that coat, which would almost have done her for an overcoat. Then they recognised that perfect proportion had given her stature and that, if the gods had made her head an inch or so more in circumference, she would have been a dwarf.

Then Hank started forward to find a tailor amongst the Chinks and returned with a slit-eyed individual who contemplated his strange customer, standing like Mr. Hyde in the garment of Dr. Jekyll, took eye measurements of the length of her limbs and the circumference of her waist and retired to the foc'sle with two pairs of white drill trousers and two coats to work his works, also some white silk pajamas and shirts, producing by the next morning an outfit which fitted, more or less. She solved the question of shoes and stockings by discarding them on deck.

That was on the morning when, across the sea to port, Cape San Lazaro showed itself and the heat-hazy opening to Magdalena Bay.

The steady nor'westerly breeze that had held all night began to flicker out at dawn; when they came up from breakfast the world had gone to sleep. From the hazy coast to the hazy horizon nothing moved but the vast marching glassy swell coming up from a thousand miles away and unruffled by the faintest breeze.

Tommie, having come on deck and taken a sniff at the glacial condition of things, curled herself in one of the deck chairs with a book. The *Wear Jack* was well provided with deck chairs and Hank, having inspected the weather, dived below and brought one up; George followed suit. Then, having placed the chairs about under the awning which had been rigged, they sat and smoked and talked, Tommie, up to her eyes in her confounded book, taking no part in the conversation.

T. C. was one of those readers who become absolutely dead to surroundings. Curled there with her nose in "Traffics and Discoveries," she looked as if you might have knicked her without waking her, and this fact somehow cast a pall over the conversation of Hank and Bud, who, after a few minutes, found their conversation beginning to dry up.

"Lord," said Hank, "I wonder how long this beastly calm's going to hold."

"Don't know," said George.

Then Candon came on deck. He had no chair. He stood with his back to the port rail cutting up some tobacco and filling a pipe.

"I wonder how long this beastly calm is going to hold," said George.

"Lord knows," said Candon.

Tommie chuckled. Something in the book had tickled her, she turned over a page rapidly and plunged deeper into oblivion like a puffin after smelts.

"What's the current taking us?" asked George.

"Maybe three knots," said Hank. "There's no saying." He yawned, then, as though the idea had just struck him, "Say—what's wrong with trying the engine?"

"It's too beastly hot for tinkering over engines," yawned George, "and B. C. says he can't get the thing to go."

"Go'n' have another try, B. C.," said Hank. "There's no use in us sitting here wagging our tails and waiting for the wind. Tell you what, I'll draw lots with you—give's a piece of paper, Bud."

George produced an old letter and Hank tore off three slips, one long and two short.

Candon, with little interest in the business, drew a short slip, George the long one.

"It's me," said George rising. "Well now, I'll just tell you, if I don't get the thing to revolute I'll stick there till I do. I'm not going to be beat by a bit of machinery." He moved towards the hatch.

"I'll go with you," said Tommie, suddenly dog's-earing a page and closing her book, as though she had been listening to the whole conversation, which, in a way, she had.

Hank and Candon were left alone and Candon took his seat in the chair vacated by George. Neither seemed in good humour; perhaps it was the heat.

From down below, through the open hatch leading to the little engine room, they could hear voices! George's voice and the voice of T. C.

Then, as they sat yawning, another sound came, faint and far away, rhythmical, ghostly.

Hank raised himself and looked. Away to the s'uth'ard, across the glassy sea, a freighter was coming up. She was a great distance off, but in the absolute stillness and across that glacial calm the thud of her propellers could be felt by the ear.

Both men left their chairs and leaned on the rail watching her.

Said Candon, after a moment's silence, "D'y' know what I've been thinking? I've been thinking we've played it pretty low-down on T. C."

"How?"

"Well, it's this way. McGinnis will be after us, sure, as soon as he can get his hoofs under him. He'll know we're making for the Bay of Whales and he'll be after us. Question is, can he get the *Heart* tinkered up in time, or would he take another boat. If he does and catches us, there's sure to be a fight. We should have told T. C. that. I thought of it this morning at breakfast."

"Well, why didn't you tell her?"

"Well, I didn't, somehow. There's another thing, we've never told her who I am. That's worried me."

"Well, it's easy enough to tell her."

"No, sir, it isn't, not by a long chalk. I almost came to it yesterday. It was when you two were down below and I had her here on deck showing her how to make a fisherman's bend. It came to me to tell her and I opened out about Vanderdecken, saying he wasn't maybe as bad as some folk painted him, then she closed me up and put the lid on."

"What did she say?"

"Said stealing was stealing and taking women's jewelry was a dirty trick."

"Why didn't you explain?"

"Because she was right. Right or wrong, how's a fellow to explain? Well, there it is. You'd better go down to her and say, 'That lad Candon's Vanderdecken and Pat McGinnis is after him and there'll maybe be a dust-up when we get down to the Bay, and there's a freighter coming along that'll take you back north and you'd better get aboard her.'"

"Me!"

"Yes, you—it's clean beyond me."

Hank watched the freighter. She was away up now out of the water and showing the white of her bridge screen. At her present speed she would soon be level with them.

"She looks to be in ballast, don't she?" said Hank.

"Yep."

"Where's she going, do you think?"

"'Frisco, sure."

"That's a long way from Los Angeles."

"Maybe, but it's nearer than the Bay o' Whales."

The freighter grew; she was making anything from twelve to fifteen knots; she would pass the *Wear Jack* and a signal would stop her as sure as a bullet through the eye will stop a man.

Then, suddenly, something that had risen to Hank's surface intelligence like a bubble, burst angrily.

"You can go down and tell her yourself," said he, "it's no affair of mine. If she wasn't fooling there with Bud, she'd have seen the ship. How'n the nation do you think I'm going to go down and give you away like that?"

Candon hung silent, as if offended with the other. He wasn't in the least. His eyes were fixed on the water over the side. Right below, in the bit of shadow cast by the ship against the morning sun, the water lay, pure emerald, and showing fathom-deep glimpses of life, scraps of fuci, hints of jelly fish and once, far down, like a moving jewel in a world of crystal, an albacore passing swift as a sword thrust.

Ahead of them on the lifting swell a turtle was sunning itself awash in the blue of that lazy silent sea, one polished plate of its carapace showing like a spot of burnished steel.

Candon found himself wondering why one plate should shine like that. It looked now like a little window in a roof, then it seemed to him that out of that window came an idea, or rather a vision. A horrible vision of the freighter going off with Tommie and vanishing beyond the northern sky-line with her. Not till that moment had he recognised that T. C. was at once the lynch-pin of their coach and the thing that had suddenly come to lend reason to his own life. His whole existence had led logically up to the Vanderdecken business and the Vanderdecken business had led to her capture and her capture had given him something to care for, not as a man cares for a girl, but more as a lonely man cares for a child or a dog. It was her small size, maybe, that clinched the thing with him and made him feel that he'd sooner do a dive overside than lose touch with her.

Hank was feeling at that moment pretty much the same. The microscopic Tommie had captured the leathery Hank as a chum.

The freighter drew on and they could see now the touch of white where the spume rose in a feather at her fore foot. It was a huge brute of a Coleman liner up from Callao or Valparaiso, a five thousand tonner with a rust-red funnel.

If they stopped her, it would be necessary to get T. C. on deck right away and the Chinks ready to man the boat. There would be scarcely time to say good-bye—besides, it was ten to one T. C. wouldn't want to go—besides she was in those togs. The freighter was abreast of them now. They watched her without a word. Suddenly a stream of bunting fluttered up and blew out on the wind of her passage. Candon shaded his eyes and looked.

"Wishing us a pleasant voyage," said Candon.

They watched the flags flutter down and the great turtle backed stern with the sunlight on it and the plumes of foam from the propellers. Then, as the wash reached them, making the *Wear Jack* groan and clatter her blocks, came a new sound, a thrud-thrud-thrud right under their feet, followed by the voice of George yelling, "Hi, you chaps, get the helm on her, engine's going."

Candon sprang to the wheel and Hank came and stood beside him.

Hank said, "That freighter must have thought us awful swine not acknowledging their signal."

"Maybe they thought right," said Candon.

At that moment, George appeared, triumphant from the engine room. "She's running a treat," said he, "and T. C.'s looking after her. What's made the cross swell?" Without waiting for an answer and at a call from Tommie, he dived below again.

Half an hour later when he came on deck, taking a look aft, George said: "Now if we hadn't an auxiliary engine and if it wasn't running well, this calm would have lasted a fortnight. Look there!"

They looked. Away to northward a vast expanse of the glassy swell had turned to a tray of smashed sapphires.

It was the breeze.

CHAPTER XXV

THEY TURN THE CORNER

THEY had given Tommie the after cabin, but this hot weather the three of them kept the deck at night so that she might have her door open, and tonight, just before dawn when the *Wear Jack* was right on to Cape St. Lucas, Candon and George were keeping watch and listening to Hank. Hank was lying on the deck with a pillow under his head, snoring. The engine had been shut off to save gasoline, and the *Wear Jack*, with a Chink at the wheel and the main boom guyed out, was sailing dead before the wind, under a million stars, through a silence broken only by the bow wash and the snores of Hank.

Candon, pacing the deck with George, was in a reflective mood.

"Wonder what that Chink's thinking about?" said he. "Home mostlike. They say every Chinaman carries China about with him in his box and unpacks it when he lights his opium pipe. Well, it's a good thing to have a home. Lord! what's the good of anything else, what's the good of working for money to spend in Chicago or N' York? I reckon there's many a millionaire in the cities, living all day in his office on pills an' pepsin, would swop his dollars for the old home if he could get it back, the old shanty near where the cows used to graze in the meadows and the fish jump in the stream, with his old dad and his mother sitting by the fire and his sister Sue playin' on the step."

"Where was your home?" asked George.

"Never had one," said Candon, "and never will."

"Oh, yes, you will."

"Don't see it. Don't see where it's to come from, even if I had the dollars. I'm a lone man. Reckon there's bucks in every herd same as me. Look at me, getting on for forty and the nearest thing to a home is a penitentiary. That's so."

"Now look here, B. C.," said George,—then he stopped dead. A sudden great uplift had come in his mind. Perhaps it was the night of stars through which they were driving or some waft from old Harley du Cane, the railway wrecker, who, still, always had his hand in his pocket for any unfortunate; perhaps he had long and sub-consciously been debating in his mind the case of Candon: who knows?

"You were going to say—?" said Candon.

"Just this," said George. "Close up on the penitentiary business. There's worse men than you in the church, B. C., or I'm a nigger. You're going to have a home yet and a jolly good one. I've got it for you."

"Where?"

"In my pocket. Fruit farming, that's your line, and a partner that can put up the dollars—that's me."

Candon was silent for a moment.

"It's good of you," said he at last, "damn good of you. I reckon I could make a business pay if it came to that, but there's more than dollars, Bud. I reckon I was born a wild duck. I've no anchor on board that wouldn't pull out of the mud first bit of wind that'd make me want to go wandering."

"I'll fix you up with an anchor," said Bud, "somehow or other. You leave things to me and trust your uncle Bud."

He was thinking of getting Candon married, somehow, to some girl. He could almost visualize her: a big, healthy, honest American girl, businesslike, with a heart the size of a cauliflower—some anchor.

"Sun's coming," said George, turning and stirring Hank awake with the point of his toe. Hank sat up yawning.

Away on the port bow, against a watery blue window of sky, Cape St. Lucas showed, its light-house winking at the dawn. Then came the clang of gulls, starting for the fishing, and moment by moment as they watched, the sea beyond the cape showed sharper, steel-blue and desolate beyond words. The north could show nothing colder, till, all at once, over the hills came colour on a suddenly materialised reef of cloud.

They held their course whilst the day grew broader and the cape fell astern; then, shifting the helm, they steered right into the eye of the sun for the coast of Mexico.

They had turned the tip of Lower California.

CHAPTER XXVI

THE BAY OF WHALES

MAGDALENA Bay, that great expanse of protected water between Punta Entrado and Santa Margarita Island, was once a great haunt of the sulphur bottom whales. Then came the shark fishers and then came the American Pacific Fleet and made a gun practice ground of it, just as they have made a speed testing ground of the Santa Barbara Channel between the Channel Islands and the coast. Maybe that drove the sulphur bottoms to go south all in a body and the more pessimistical ones to commit suicide in a bunch, and all on the same day in the bay once known as the Bay of Jaures and now as the Bay of Whales. For the bones seem all of the same date, ghost-white, calcined by sun and worn by the moving sands that cover them and uncover them and the winds that drive the sands.

Another thing, you find them almost to the foot of the low cliffs that ring the bay. How has this happened? The wind. The wind that can lift as well as drift, the wind that is always redisposing the sands.

The bay stretches for a distance of four miles between horn and horn; the water is strewn with reefs visible at low tide. Emerald shallows and sapphire depths and foam lines and snow of gulls all show more beautiful than any picture; and beyond lie the sands and the cliffs and the country desolate as when Jaures first sighted it. Near the centre of the beach, at the sea edge, stands a great rock shaped like a pulpit.

"That's the bay," said Candon, pointing ahead.

It was noon and the *Wear Jack*, with all plain sail set, was driving straight for a great blue break in the reefs, Hank at the helm and Candon giving directions. The Chinks were all on deck, gathered forward, their faces turned shoreward, gazing at the land almost with interest.

"Where are the whales?" asked Tommie suddenly. "You said it was all covered with the skeletons of whales."

"You'll see them quick enough," said Candon. "Port, steady so."

The rip of the outgoing tide was making a lather round the reef spurs. Ahead the diamond-bright dead blue water showed up to a line where it suddenly turned to emerald.

"It's twenty fathoms up to there," said Candon, "and then the sands take hold. I'm anchoring somewhere about here. It's a good bottom. Make ready with the anchor there!"

He held on for another minute or so, then the wind spilled from the sails and the anchor fell in fifteen fathom water and nearly half a mile from the shore.

The boat was got over, with two Chinks to do the rowing, and they started, Candon steering.

"Where's the whales?" asked Tommie.

They were almost on to the beach now and there lay the sands singing to the sun and wind. Miles and miles of sand, with ponds of mirage to the south, and gulls strutting on the uncovered beach; a vast desolation, with, far overhead, just a dot in the blue, an eagle from the hills of Sinaloa. An eagle so high as to be all but invisible, whose eyes could yet number the shells on the beach and the movement of the smallest crab. But where were the whales?

T. C. had once seen a whale's skeleton in a museum, set up and articulated. Her vivid imagination had pictured a beach covered with whale skeletons just like that, and, instead of thanking providence for the absence of such a boneyard, her mind grumbled. She was wearing one of Bud's superfluous panamas and she took it off and put it on again.

As they landed close to the pulpit rock Hank said nothing, George said nothing, Candon, visibly disturbed, looked north and south. Here but a short time ago had been ribs lying about like great bent staves, skulls, vertebræ. Here to-day there was nothing but sand.

He did not know that a fortnight ago a south wind had "moved the beach," bringing up hundreds of thousands of tons of sand not only from the south end but from the bay beyond; that in a month more, maybe, a north wind would move the beach, sending the sand back home; that only between the winds the bones were laid fully bare. No storm was required to do the work, just a steady driving wind sifting, sifting, sifting for days and days.

The fact that the beach seemed higher just here suddenly brought the truth to Candon.

"Boys," said he, "it's the sand."

No one spoke for a moment under the frost that had fallen on them. Then Hank said, "Sure you've struck the right bay?"

Like Tommie, he had pictured entire skeletons, not bones and skulls lying flat and easily sanded over.

"Sure. It's the sand has lifted over them."

Scarcely had he spoken when a thunderbolt fell into the shallows a cable length away from the shore. It was the eagle. In a moment it rose, a fish in its talons, and went climbing the air to seaward, and then up a vast spiral stairs in the blue, and then, like an arrow, away to the far-off hills.

It was like an underscore to the desolation of this place, where man was disregarded if not unknown.

"Well," said George, coming back to things, "the bones aren't any use anyway. Let's start for the boodle. Strike out for the cache, B. C."

They turned, following their leader, and made diagonally for the cliffs to the north. Candon walked heavily, a vague suspicion filling his mind that Hank and George held something more in reservation than mere disappointment over absent skeletons. The odious thought that they might suspect him of being a fraud came to him as he walked, but he had little time for self communing. Something worse was in store, and he saw it now, and wondered at his stupidity in not having seen it before.

Amongst the implements of the expedition two spades had been brought. The Chinks carried these spades. They brought up the rear of the procession, silent, imperturbable, apparently incurious. They would not do the digging when the moment came. Candon and Hank, or George would be easily able to negotiate the few feet of hard sand that covered the treasure. The Chinks just carried the spades. Candon stopped dead all of a sudden. Then he went on, quickening his pace almost to a run. The booty had been buried at a place easily recognisable, on the southern side of a little out-jut of the cliff and about ten feet from an issue of water that came clear and cold and bright through a crack in the cliff face.

The issue was still there, but it was far lower than before; the sand had risen. The wind had done its work and five feet or more of new sand lay upon the cache. It ran up the cliff face like a snow drift. Five or six feet of pliable sand that seemed an almost impassable barrier. The big man folded his arms and stood for a moment dumb. Then he laughed.

"Boys," said he, "I'm a fraud."

No answer came but the wash of the little waves on the beach and far gull voices from the south. He turned about fiercely.

"I've led you wrong. I've fooled you, but it's not me. It's my pardner. It's the sand. Sand. That's me and all my work. All I've ever stood on, sand. Sand. Six foot deep."

"For the land's sake, B. C.," cried Hank, "get a clutch on yourself. What's wrong with you anyhow?"

"He means the sand has covered the cache," said the steady voice of Tommie.

Candon did not look at her. It seemed to him just then, in that moment of disappointment, that Fate was carefully explaining to him the futility of his works and his life, and in an immeasurably short space of time all sorts of little details, from his Alaskan experiences to his absurd rescue of Tommie, all sorts of weaknesses, from his enjoyment of robbery to his inaction in letting that freighter pass, rose before him. He struggled to find more words.

"It's just me," said he, and fell dumb and brooding.

"Well," said George, "it's a long way to come—to be fooled like this—but there's an end of it. How many men would it take to move that stuff?"

"Six foot of sand and square yards of surface; it would take a steam dredger," said Hank, in a hard voice.

Tommie's eyes were fixed on Candon. She knew little of the whole thing, but she knew suffering when she saw it. From what he had said and from his attitude, she could almost read Candon's thoughts. The movie business is a teacher of dumb expression.

"D'you mean to say you're going to turn this down?" asked Tommie.

"What's the good?" said George. He was feeling just as Hank felt. The absence of whales' bones, the flatness of landing on an ordinary beach where they had expected to see strange sights, had deflated them both. They did not doubt the bona fides of B. C., but as a medicine man he was at a discount.

They saw before them hopeless digging. The thing was not hopeless, but in that moment of defection and disappointment it seemed impossible.

"Well," said Tommie, "next time I start on a show of this kind, I'll take girls along—that's all I've got to say."

In the dead silence following this bomb-shell, Candon looked up and found himself looking straight into the eyes of the redoubtable T. C.

"Talk of sands," she went on, talking to him and seeming to disregard the others, "and all your life has been sands and that nonsense, why it's the sand in a man that makes him. Anyhow, I've not come all this distance to go back without having a try. Aren't you going to dig?"

The scorn in her tone had no equivalent in her mind, no more than the spur on a rider's heel has to do with his mentality. She was out to save B. C. from himself. Also, although she did not care a button for the hidden "boodle," her whole soul resented turning back when on the spot.

Candon, standing before her like a chidden child, seemed to flush under his tan, then his eyes turned to Hank.

"Lord! let's dig," suddenly said Hank. "Let's have a try anyhow, if it takes a month." He stopped and stared at the hopeless looking task before him. "We'll get the whole of the Chinks to help—"

"Chinks!" said Candon, suddenly coming back to his old self in a snap. "This is white men's work—I brought you here and I'll do it myself if I have to dig with my hands. It's there, and we've got to get it."

"I'll help," said Tommie.

"Well, I reckon we'll all help," said George, unenthusiastically.

It was a strange fact that, of the three men, Tommie had least power over George du Cane. Less attraction for him maybe, even though the very clothes on her back were his.

CHAPTER XXVII

THE CONFESSION

THE size of the task was apparent to all of them, but to none more clearly than Candon.

First of all, reckoning to deal with hard stuff, he had brought spades, not shovels. The bundle had been buried hurriedly; even under the best conditions he would have had to turn over many square feet of stuff to find it. Then this soft fickle sand was a terrible material to work on; it was like trying to shovel away water, almost. But the most daunting thing to him was the fact that fate had induced him to make the cache on the south side of the out-jut of cliff instead of the north, for the south wind, blowing up from the bay beyond, had added feet to the depth to be dealt with, just as a wind drifts snow against any obstruction. The sand level on the north of the jut was much lower, and it was not drifted. Then there was the question of time. Given time enough the McGinnis crowd would surely arrive, if he knew anything of them, and there would be a fight. And there was the question of Tommie.

This last consideration only came to him now on top of her words, "I'll help." He stood for a moment plunged back into thought. Then he turned to the others.

"Boys, I reckon I've been talking through my hat. White man or yellow man it's all the same, we'll all have to take our turn. Back with you, you two, to the ship and get canvas enough for tents. We'll want three. Grub, too; we'll want enough for a week. Leave two Chinks to look after the schooner and try to get some boarding to make extra shovels, as much as you can, for we'll want some to shore up the sand. We've got to camp here right on our work."

"Sure," said Hank. "Come along, Bud, we'll fetch the truck." They turned towards the boat.

"I'll go with you," said Tommie, "I want to fetch my book."

"I'd rather you didn't," said Candon, "I want you to help me here."

"Me!" said Tommie surprised.

"Yes—if you don't mind."

"All right," said she. Then to Hank, "You'll find the book in my bunk, and fetch me my tooth brush, will you—and that hair brush and my pyjamas, if we've got to camp."

"Right," said Hank, "you trust me."

They shoved off, and to George, as he looked back, the huge figure of Candon and the little figure of his companion seemed strange standing side by side on that desolate beach. Stranger even than the whales' skeletons that had vanished.

The wind had veered to the west and freshened, blowing in cool from the sea.

"Well," said Tommie after they had watched the boat half way to the schooner, "what are you going to do now? What did you want me for?"

"I want to have a word with you," said Candon. "S'pose we sit down. It's fresh and breezy here and I can think better sitting down than standing up. I'm bothered at your being dragged into this business, and that's the truth, and I've things to tell you." They sat down and the big man took his pipe from his pocket and filled it in a leisurely and far-away manner, absolutely automatically.

Tommie watched him, vastly interested all of a sudden.

"It's this way," said he, "I got rid of the other chaps so's I could get you alone, and I'm not going one peg further in this business till you know all about me and the chances you're running. Y' remember one day on deck I was talking to you about that chap Vanderdecken?"

"Yes."

"Well, I'm Vanderdecken."

"You're which?"

"I'm Vanderdecken. The swab that pirated those yachts."

"You!" said Tommie.

"Yes. I'm the swab."

A long pause followed this definite statement. The gulls cried and the waves broke. Tommie, leaning on her elbow and watching the breaking waves, seemed trying to adjust her mind to this idea and failing utterly. She was not considering the question of how Vanderdecken, who was being chased by Hank and George, had managed to be in partners with them; she was up against the great fact that Candon was a robber. It seemed impossible to her, yet he said so.

"But what made you *do* it?" she cried, suddenly sitting up and looking straight at him.

"I didn't start to do it," said he, throwing the unlit pipe beside him on the sand. "All the same I did it, and I'll tell you how it was." He sat up and holding his knees started to talk, telling her the whole business.

It sounded worse than when he told Hank and George, for he gave nothing in extenuation, just the hard bricks. But hard bricks were good enough for Tommie; she could build better with them and quicker than if he had handed her out ornamental tiles to be inserted at given positions.

When he had done talking and when she had done building her edifice from his words, she shook her head over it. It wasn't straight. In some ways it pleased her, as, for instance, the liquor business. She had sympathy with that, but the larceny appealed to her not as an act of piracy but theft. T. C. would have been smothered in a judge's wig, but she would have made an excellent judge for all that. Candon was now clearly before her, the man and his actions; he had been frank as day with her, he was a repentant sinner, and to cap all he had saved her, at all events in intention, from Chinese slavers. His size and his sailor simplicity appealed to her.

All the same, her sense of right refused to be stirred by the blue eyes of Candon, by his size, his simplicity, his patent daring, by the something or other that made her like him even better than Hank or George, by the fact that he had carried her off on his shoulder against her will and in the face of destruction—and absurdity.

"You shouldn't have done it," said Tommie. "I don't want to rub it in, but you shouldn't. You shouldn't have got mixed up with that McGinnis crowd. What made you?"

"You've put your finger on it," said Candon. "I don't know what made me. Want of steering."

"Well," said Tommie, "you wish you hadn't, don't you?"

"You bet."

"Well then, you're half out of the hole. D'you ever say your prayers?"

"Me! no—" Candon laughed. "Lord, no—I've never been given that way."

"Maybe if you had you wouldn't have got into this hole—or maybe you would. No telling," said Tommie. "I'm no praying beetle myself, but I regularly ask the Lord for protection. You want it in the movies. Dope and a broken neck is what I'm afraid of. I don't mind being killed, but I don't want to be killed suddenly or fall for cocaine or whisky, the way some do. Well, I guess work is praying sometimes and I shouldn't wonder but you'll have some praying to do with your fists, getting the sand off that stuff. And when you've sent it back to its owners, you'll have prayed yourself clear—that's my 'pinion."

"I've got something else to tell you," said Candon, "I reckon you don't know me yet, anyhow you've got to have the lot now I've begun."

"Spit it out," said the confessor, a bit uneasy in her mind at this new development and the serious tone of the other.

"I told the boys there was a black streak in me. And there is. I let you down."

"Let me down?"

"Yep. D'you remember when you were tinkering at the engine that day the calm took us?"

"Yes."

"Well, a big freighter passed within hail and I let her go."

"Well, what about it?"

"I should have stopped her so that you might have got back to 'Frisco."

"But I didn't want to go to 'Frisco."

"Why, you said the day we first had you on board that you could get back on some ship."

"Oh, did I? I'd forgot—well, I wouldn't have gone in the freighter, to 'Frisco of all places."

"I didn't know that. From what you said I should have stopped her."

"Why didn't you?"

"Well," said he, "I didn't want to lose you. Hank and me didn't want you to go off and leave us, you'd been such a good chum."

"Well, forget it. I didn't want to leave you, either. Not me! Why, this trip is the best holiday I've had for years. If that's all you have to bother about, forget it."

"There's something else," said he. "The McGinnis crowd is pretty sure to blow along down after us and there'll be a fight, sure. You see, we're held here by that sand; that will give them time to get on our tracks."

"If they come, we'll have to fight them," said Tommie. "But, if you ask me, I don't think there's much fight in that lot, by what you say of them."

"They're toughs, all the same. I'm telling you, and I want you to choose right now—we can stay here and risk it, or push out and away back and put you down at Santa Barbara, give us the word."

Tommie considered deeply for a moment. Then she said: "I'm not afraid. I reckon we can match them if it comes to scratching. No, we'll stick. You see, there's two things—you can't put me back in Santa Barbara without the whole of this business coming out and Hank Fisher and Bud du Cane being guyed to death. Your ship is known, Althusen and that lot will give evidence—you can't put me back out of the *Wear Jack* anyhow."

"Then how are you to get back?" asked Candon.

"I've been trying to think that long enough," said Tommie. "You remember the rat in the flower pot—something or another will turn up, or I'll have to do some more thinking."

"Do you know what I'm thinking?" asked Candon. "I'm thinking there's not many would stick this out just to save a couple of men from being guyed."

"Maybe—I don't know. Anyhow the other thing is I want to see the end of this business and that stuff got out of the sand and handed back to its owners. Lord, can't you see? If we turned back now we'd be quitters, and I don't know what you'd do with yourself; but I tell you what I'd do with myself, I'd take to making lace for a living—or go as mother's help—paugh!"

"God!" said Candon, "give me your fist."

Tommie held out her fist and they shook.

CHAPTER XXVIII

HANK

HANK, as before mentioned, was a man of resource; there was nothing much he could not do with his hands backed by his head. In two hours on board the *Wear Jack* he had found the materials for and constructed three tent poles; in the sail room, and by sacrificing the awning, he had obtained the necessary canvas; ropes and pegs evolved themselves from nowhere as if by magic. Then in some way, and from the interior of the *Wear Jack*, he managed to get planking, not much, but enough for his purpose. Whilst he worked on these matters, George superintended the removal of stores, bully beef, canned tomatoes, canned kippered herrings, biscuits, butter, tea, condensed milk, rice. He sent two Chinks ashore with a boat-load; then, when they came back, the rest of the stuff was loaded into the boat, together with the tent poles and canvas and blankets. Last came a small bundle containing Tommie's night things and tooth brush. Then they pushed off.

Candon helped in the unloading of the boat and then they set to raising the tents.

In this section of the bay there were two breaks in the line of cliffs, a north and a south break. Hank drew the line of the tents between the breaks and at right angles to the cliffs, so as to escape, as much as possible, the hot land wind when it blew. Also he put a long distance between each tent. Tommie's was nearest the cliffs, the Chinks' nearest the sea. By sunset the canvas was up, a fire lit, a beaker filled with fresh water from the issue in the cliff and the stores piled to leeward of the middle tent. Hank had even brought mosquito netting and a plan for using it in the tents. He seemed to have forgotten nothing, till Tommie opened her bundle.

"Where's my book?" asked Tommie.

"Blest if I haven't forgot it!" cried Hank. "Chucklehead—say! I'll put off right now and fetch it."

"Oh, it'll wait," said the other. "I guess I'll be busy enough for a while not to want books. You can fetch it tomorrow."

If Hank had known the consequences of delay, he would have fetched it there and then, but he didn't. He went to attend to the fire. The fire was built of dry seaweed, bits of a broken-up packing case and fragments of wreck wood, and when the kettle was boiled over it and tea made, the sun had set and the stars were looking down on the beach.

After supper Tommie went off to her tent, leaving the men to smoke. The two Chinks, who had built a microscopic fire of their own, were seated close to it talking, maybe of China and home. The wind had died out and through the warm night the sound of the waves all down the beach came like a lullaby.

Hank was giving his ideas of how they should start in the morning attacking the sand, when Candon, who had been smoking silently, suddenly cut in.

"I've told her," said Candon.

"What you say?" asked Hank.

"I've told her all about myself and who I am, and the chances, told her when you chaps went off for the stores. Told her it's possible McGinnis may light down on us before we've done, seeing the work before us on that sand, and there'll maybe be fighting she oughtn't to be mixed up in."

"B'gosh!" said Hank. "I never thought of that. What did she say?"

"Oh, she said, 'Let him come.' Wouldn't listen to anything about turning back, said we'd be quitters if we dropped it now."

"Lord, she's a peach."

"She's more than that," said Candon. "Well, I'm going for a breather before turning in." He tapped his pipe out and, rising, walked off down along the sea edge.

George laughed. He was laughing at the size of Candon compared to the size of Tommie, and the quaint idea that had suddenly come to him, the idea that Candon had suddenly become gone on her.

George could view the matter in a detached way, for though T. C. appealed to him as an individual, he scarcely considered her as a girl.

A lot of little signs and symptoms collected themselves together in his head, capped by the tone of those words, "She's more than that." Yes, it was highly probable that the heart punch had come to B. C. Why not? Tommie as an anchor wasn't much, as far as size went, yet as far as character and heart—who could tell? All the indications were in her favour.

"She's a peach," murmured Hank, half aloud, half to himself.

Hullo, thought George, has old Hank gone bughouse on her too! Then aloud: "You mean Tommie?"

"Yep."

"Oh, she's not so bad."

"And I went and forgot her book! Bud, d'you remember to-day, when we were all standing like a lot of lost hoodlums, going to turn our backs on this proposition, and the way she yanked us round? It came on me then."

"What?"

"I dunno. Bud, say—"

"Yes?"

"She's great. It came on me to-day like a belt on the head with a sandbag. It came to me before. Remember the day she was first aboard and wouldn't put back, wanting to save our faces? Well, that hit me, but the jaw punch got me to-day, and just now when she trundled off to her tent, lugging that blanket behind her, I seemed to get one in the solar plexus that near sent me through the ropes. Bud, I'm on my back, being counted out."

"Oh, talk sense," said Bud. "We've too much work on hand to be carrying on with girls. Tie a knot in it, Hank, till we're clear of this place, anyhow. Besides it's ten to one there's some other chap after her."

A form loomed up coming towards them. It was Candon.

CHAPTER XXIX

THE SAND

AT seven the next morning the digging began. At six, when Hank turned out of the tent, the aspect of the beach had changed. A north wind, rising before midnight, had blown steadily and strongly unheard and unheeded by the snoring sleepers in the tents. It died out after dawn.

Hank called George to look. Here and there away across the sands white spots were visible, some like the tops of gigantic mushrooms. One quite close to them showed as the top of a whale's skull. Further on a huge rib hinted of itself. There were little sand-drifts on the windward side of the tents.

"Wind's been shifting the sand," said George, "it's all over me." His hair was full of sand and his pockets. Hank was in the same condition. Tommie came out of her tent blinking at the sun.

"Say, I'm all sand," cried Tommie.

"Wind's been blowing," said Hank; "look at the bones."

The sand seemed lower over the cache.

Candon gave it as his opinion that it was at least a foot lower. Then without more ado they began to dig, using the two spades and one of the shovels improvised by Hank.

Candon, Hank and one of the Chinks were the diggers. They had divided themselves into two gangs, George, Tommie, and the other Chink forming the second gang; and they, having seen the work started, went off to prepare breakfast.

After breakfast they started again, working in two shifts of half an hour each, and keeping it up till eleven. Then they knocked off, fagged out but somehow happy. The middle of the day was too hot for work and after dinner they slept till three, knocking off finally somewhere about six. A hole ten feet broad from north to south, eight feet from east to west, and nearly three feet deep was the result of their work, the excavated stuff being banked north and south, so that if the wind blew up from either quarter, there would be less drift of sand into the hole. Hank watered these banks as far as he could with water from the spring in the cliff to make the sand "stay put"; then they went off to supper.

T. C. had worked in her way as hard as any of them, taking as a sort of personal insult any suggestion that she was overdoing herself. Dog-tired now, she was seated on the sand by the middle tent reading an old Chicago *Tribune* that George had brought ashore, whilst the others prepared supper.

"Lord," said Hank, as he knelt building up the fire. "If I haven't forgot to send for your book." He looked towards the boat on the beach and half rose to his feet.

"I'm not wanting it," said Tommie. "This is good enough for me, I'm too tired for books—tea's what I want."

She dived into the paper again, emerging when supper was announced with the gist of an article on the League of Nations between her teeth. T. C. had strong political opinions, and her own ideas about the League of Nations. She did not favour the League and said so.

Hank, opening a can of salmon and hit in his ideals, forgot it, waved it in the air and started to do battle with Tommie. That was Hank all over; heart-punched, lying on his back with Cupid counting him out, he saw for a moment only the banner of universal peace and brotherhood waving above him.

"But it isn't so," cried Hank. "There's no Monroe doctrines in morality. America can't sit scratching herself when others are up and doing. Why the nations have got war down, down, right now, kicking under the blanket, and it only wants America to sit on her head to *keep* her down."

"America's got to be strong before she does anything," fired Tommie. "How's she to be strong if a lot of foreigners sitting in Geneva can tell her to do this or that? Why they'd cut her fists off."

"Strong," cried Hank. "Why armies and navies aren't strength. Love of man for man—"

"Mean to tell me you could love Turks?"

"Ain't talking of Turks."

"Greeks then—Portugueses—say, tell me straight—do you love niggers?"

The sight of Tommie "het up" and with sparkling eyes gave the struggling hero such another heart punch that he collapsed, lost sight of the banner of brotherhood and went on opening the can of salmon.

"Maybe I'm wrong and maybe you're right," said he, "it's a big question. Pass me that plate, will you, Bud?"

Candon had said nothing. He had deserted his co-idealist like a skunk, and seemed engaged in re-reviewing the League of Nations by the light of Tommie.

Half an hour after supper the whole lot of them were snoring in their tents, pole-axed by sleep.

CHAPTER XXX

STRANGERS ON THE BEACH

NEXT day passed in labour, another two feet being added to the depth.

At ten o'clock on the morning after as the Tommie-Chink-Bud shift were taking on digging, Hank, shaking sand from his clothes, called out to the others to look.

Down from the southern defile in the cliffs a small procession was coming on to the beach. First came a man in a broad-brimmed hat, then another leading a mule, and another following after.

"Mexicans," said George.

"Sure," said Hank. "Look! they've seen us, they've stopped, now they're going on, right down to the sea edge. Wonder what they're after?"

The Mexicans, having reached the sea edge, began to wander along it coming in the direction of the tents. Every now and then they stopped to gather something.

"Seaweed," said Hank. "Look, they are shoving it into a sack on the mule."

"Well, come on," said Tommie. She jumped into the sand pit and began to dig, Bud and the Chink following her. Hank rolling a cigarette, sat down and watched the seaweed gatherers.

The tide was half out and they were following it, walking along the extreme edge of the water. Then he saw them stop and take something from the mule's back.

"Shovels," said Hank to himself. As chief engineer of the business, Hank, from the first, had been impressed by the fact that the deeper they went the harder the work would be, simply because the sand had to be flung out of the pit. The first few feet in depth it was easy enough, but the depth already gained was beginning to tell, and the banks of excavated stuff to north and south made matters worse by increasing the height over which the sand had to be flung.

"B. C.!" suddenly cried Hank, springing to his feet. "Shovels!"

Candon, who was lying on his back with his hat over his face, resting for a moment, sat up.

Hank was gone, running full speed and whooping as he ran.

He reached the sea edge and caught up with the beach-combers who were digging for huge clams just when a bank of sand and mud touched the true sand. Close to them now, they showed up as three tanned, lean, hard-bitten individuals, carrying big satisfactory heart-shaped Mexican shovels, and looking all nerves and sinews, with faces expressionless as the face of the mule that stood by with its two sacks bulging, one evidently with provender, the other with gathered sea-weed.

"Hi, you jossers," cried Hank, "want a job, hey? Mucho plenty dollars, dig for Americanos." He made movements as of digging and pointed towards the sand hole.

"No intende," replied the tallest of the three.

"Come on," said Hank, taking the long man by the arm and leading the way. He had remembered that Candon said he could talk Spanish.

The others were all out of the sand hole watching, and halfway up Candon and George joined Hank.

"Here's your dredging machine," cried Hank. "Look at the shovels, ain't they lovely? Get at them, B. C., and ask their terms."

Candon spoke with the long man, seeming to explain matters.

"Five dollars a day each," said Candon. "They say they'll work all day for that."

"Fifteen dollars," said Hank. "Take'em on, it's cheap. We can get rid of them before we strike the stuff, take'em on for one day, anyhow."

Candon concluded the bargain. Then he led the beach-combers to the hole and explained matters. They understood, then, having consulted together like experts, they took the matter into their own hands, asking only that the others should set to work and remove the banks of refuse to north and south of the hole.

"Well," said Hank as they sat at dinner that day, "give me Mexicans for work. A raft of niggers couldn't have moved the dirt quicker'n those chaps. Why, we'll be down to bed rock by to-night."

"I gingered them up," said Candon, "told them if they got down to what I wanted to find by tonight, I'd give them ten dollars extra apiece. But they won't do it."

By six o'clock that evening, however, the job was nearly done. Candon reckoned that only a few hours more work would find the stuff, unless a heavy wind blew up in the night and spoiled things.

He paid the hired men off with dollars supplied by George and then they sat down to supper, the beach-combers camping near by and having the time of their lives with canned salmon, ship's bread and peaches supplied for nothing.

Tommie had fallen in love with the mule. It had eaten half a Chicago *Tribune* blowing about on the sands and she was feeding it now with wafers, which the brute took in a gingerly and delicate manner, as though chicken and asparagus had been its up-bringing, instead of old gasoline cans and esparto grass.

"She's made friends with that mule," said George.

"She's made friends with Satan," said Hank. "Look at her talking to those greasers as if she knew their lingo."

"She's making them laugh," said Candon.

An hour after supper the beach was at peace. Even the mule had fallen into the frame of the picture.

It was lying down by its sleeping masters. Away out across the water, the amber light of the *Wear Jack* showed beneath the stars.

An hour passed. Then things changed. The mule was lying dreaming, maybe, of more wafers, and in the starlight, like shadows, the forms of the three Mexicans, each with a shovel over its shoulder, were passing towards the sand-hole.

CHAPTER XXXI

"TOMMIE'S GONE!"

"ROUSE up, Hank!"

Hank, snoring on his back, flung out his arms, opened his eyes, yawned and stared at the beautiful blazing morning visible through the tent opening.

"Lord! it's good to be alive!" said Hank. He dressed and came out.

Candon was tinkering at the fire. The mule, on its feet now, was standing, whilst Tommie was feeding it with dried grass taken from the provender bag, the Mexicans, sitting like tired men, were smoking cigarettes, whilst the four mile beach sang to the crystal waves and the white gulls laughed.

It was a pretty picture.

Tommie came running to the heap of stores by the middle tent, chose a couple of tins, wrapped up some biscuits in a bit of newspaper and presented the lot to the Mexicans.

"They look so tired," said she, as they sat down to breakfast.

"Well they ought to be," said Hank, "seeing the way they've been digging. Boys, I reckon they ought to have a bonus."

"They've had fifteen dollars," said the practical George, "and their grub."

"Maybe," said Hank, "but they've done fifty dollars' worth of work, seeing how we're placed. I vote we give them five dollars extra."

"I'm with you," said Candon.

"Ten," said Tommie.

"I've only a ten dollar bill left on me," said George. "Don't matter, give it to them."

Tommie took the note and, leaving her breakfast, tripped over to the Mexicans. Then she came back.

Half an hour later, armed only with the spades and Hank's improvised shovel, they set to work.

"Let's borrow the greasers' shovels," said George.

"I'd rather not," said Candon, "they'll be going off the beach soon, and I'd rather they weren't here when we strike the stuff, we'll be soon on it now."

"What's the matter with the sand?" asked Hank as he contemplated the floor of the hole. "Looks as if it had been beaten down with a shovel."

"Shovel—nothing—" said George, "it's their flat feet, come on!"

By half past eleven o'clock, Candon reckoned that the depth required had been reached if not passed.

"We'll get it this evening," said he, "as sure's my name's Bob Candon."

"Hope so," said George.

As they turned to the tents for dinner and siesta, they found that the Mexicans were still on the beach a bit to the southward, strolling along by the sea edge. Then they came back northwards.

"I wish those greasers would go," said George.

When they turned in for the mid-day siesta, the beach-combers seemed to have made a little camp for the purpose of rest and cigarette smoking half-way between the sea edge and the southern defile in the cliffs.

George slept, at first the sleep of the just, then began the sleep of canned kippered herrings and 80° in the shade. Tyrebuck was buried alive somewhere on the beach and they were trying to locate him without treading on him; then, having seemingly given up this quest, they were seated playing cards with Hank's late partner, the lady who could put a whole potato in her mouth. They were playing a new sort of game which the ingenious Hank had invented and which he called Back to Front. That is to say they were holding their cards so that each player could only see the backs of his own hand and the fronts of his partner's hand. It was bridge, moreover, and they were playing for potato points. How long this extremely intellectual game lasted, it is impossible to say. It was suddenly interrupted.

Hank outside the tent had seized his foot and seemed trying to pull his leg off.

"Come out!" cried Hank. "She's gone!"

"Gone! Who's gone?"

"Tommie. They've stolen her."

Candon, already awakened and out, was running around looking at the sand as if hunting her foot steps.

The raving Hank explained that, unable to sleep, he had come out and found the Mexicans gone. Some premonition of evil had made him glance at Tommie's tent opening. Not being able to see her, he looked closer. She was gone. They had stolen her.

"After them!" cried George.

Aroused from a fantastic dream he found himself faced with something almost equally fantastic. The size of Tommie made a lot of things possible. Visions of her, captured and strangled and stuffed into one of the bags on the mule's back, rose before him, though why or for what purpose the greasers should commit such an act was not clear.

The going was hard over the sand till they reached the defile in the cliffs towards which the mule tracks seemed to lead. Here the way led gently uphill over broken rocky ground till they reached a low plateau where, under the unchanging sunlight, the landscape lay spread in humps and hollows to the hills away to the east. Rock, sagebrush and sand, cactus, sand, sagebrush, it lay before them; but of Tommie, the mule or her captors, there was no trace or sign. The sand here was no use for tracking purposes, it was beach sand blown up by west winds and lay only in places, rock was the true floor, rock rising sometimes six feet in camel humps obstructing the view.

Candon climbed one of these kopjes, shaded his eyes and looked. Then he gave a shout.

"Got 'em," cried Candon, "right ahead. After me, boys!"

He came tumbling down and started at full speed, taking a track that led due east between the hillocks, till, rounding a boulder, away ahead of them, they saw the mule and its companions slowly winding their way in a south-easterly direction—but not a trace of Tommie.

They closed up rapidly, the Mexicans turned at the shout of Hank, then, as if a bomb shell had burst amongst them, they scattered, leaving the mule to its fate and running south, sou'east and east.

"Mule first," cried Hank.

Through the canvas of the great bulging sack of sea-weed on the mule's back, he could see the small corpse of Tommie, strangled, maybe, doubled up, done for.

The mule, left to itself, had begun to feed on a patch of grass as tough looking as bow-string hemp. It cocked an eye at the oncomers and continued feeding till they got close up to it.

"Look out!" yelled Hank.

The heels of the brute had missed him by inches.

They scattered, picking up rocks by instinct and instinctively planning and carrying out their attack without word of common counsel. It was the primitive man, no doubt, aroused by rage; at all events the mule, mechanically grazing, got, next moment, a whack on its rump with a rock that made it squeal and wheel only to get another on its flank. It flung its heels up as if trying to kick heaven.

"Stand clear," cried Hank. The sack, provender and shovels had fallen to the ground and the mule, seeing an open course and impelled by another rock, was off.

Hank flung himself on the sack. There was no Tommie in it, only seaweed. Candon, recognising this, made off, running after the Mexicans, but something was protruding from the provender bag that was not provender. Hank pulled it out. It was a parcel done up in oil cloth and tied clumsily with tarred string.

"Lord!" cried George. "The boodle!"

The shock of the discovery almost made them forget Tommie for a moment.

"Hounds," said Hank. "They must have been digging last night after we turned in."

"And they've opened it," said George. "Look at the way it's tied up again—and that knot's a granny. Oh, damn! What's the use of bothering? We haven't got her. Hank, clutch a hold of the damned thing and hide it somewhere and come on. Scatter and hunt."

Candon had made off due east. They heard his voice shouting, "Hi, there, hi there! Tommie! Ahoy there!" Then Hank, throwing the parcel at the foot of a prominent upstanding rock, made off south and Bud north.

The eagle of the Simaloa hills, having fed its young that morning, had returned to its watch tower and from there she saw the hunt. She saw Hank overtaking and kicking a Mexican, Bud chasing another Mexican, Candon pursuing a third. Philosophising, perhaps, on the craziness of human beings, she saw the chase of the Mexicans relinquished and the pursuers each now seemingly in pursuit of something else.

An hour later Hank, returning to the rock where he had flung the bundle, found Bud.

"She's not here," said Hank, "but she can't be anywhere else—I'm done—there's nothing for it but to hike back and get all the Chinks and comb this place. It's not the Mexicans. She's maybe wandered out here alone and fallen off a rock or into a hole or got sunstroke. Come on and fetch the Chinks."

"Where's B. C.?"

"I dunno. Chasing away there somewhere—come on."

He caught up the bundle and they started, the most dejected pair of human beings in Mexico at that moment. They couldn't speak. They came through the defile in the cliffs and there on the sands lay the new beached boat, and on the sands the tents, and half in and out of her tent, sitting with her head in the shade and her feet in the sun, Tommie reading a book.

Hank dropped the bundle and ran towards her, shouting as he ran and waving his arms.

CHAPTER XXXII

THE RETURN OF CANDON

BUD saw her spring up, evidently fancying some danger was upon them, then he saw Hank seizing her and jumping her round in a sort of dance.

When he reached them, Hank had flung himself down on the sand and was laughing.

"He's gone crazy," said Tommie, laughing despite herself. "Where on earth you been?"

"Been!" cried George. "Hunting Mexico for you, thinking you were lost. Where have *you* been?"

"Me—only to get my book. I took the boat when you two were asleep and I got back here a few minutes ago and found you all gone."

"Well," said Bud, sitting down on the sand. "I was asleep when Hank pulled me out by the leg, saying you were gone and the Mexicans had stolen you, then we all started off to chase them and hunt for you."

"But didn't you see the boat was gone?" asked she.

"I only saw you were gone," said Hank, "and the Mexicans."

"Hank told us they'd boned you and made off with you," put in George. "I took it for gospel and started right off."

Hank snorted. "What else was a body to think. It gets me. Say, people, what's wrong with this cruise anyhow. Look at it."

The idea that his own frightful imagination had not only launched the whole expedition, but had dragged Tommie in, broken up a picture show and wrecked a junk, to say nothing of the latter business, never dawned on him or his companions, nor the premonition that his imagination had not done with them yet.

"Where's B. C.?" asked Tommie suddenly.

"Hunting away still," replied George.

"What's in that bundle?"

"Oh, the bundle—why it's the boodle; the greasers must have dug it up, for we found it in the sack on the mule."

"The jewels!"

"Yep."

"*My!*" said Tommie, her eyes wide and the colour coming to her cheeks. "*Why* didn't you tell me?" She seized on it.

"I'll help," said Hank, "you'll dirty your fingers with the string."

"Bother my fingers."

She had the string off and then, unwrapping the oilskin cover, came on sack cloth. Opening this unskilfully the whole contents shot out on her knees and the sand. Diamond rings, ten silver spoons, a diamond necklace, blazing, huge and vulgar, a diamond hair ornament like a tiara, a ring set with rubies, another with emeralds, a woman's wrist watch set with diamonds, and a silver pepper pot. Twenty or thirty thousand dollars' worth of plunder, at least, and shouting with individuality. One could see the fat woman who once wore the necklace and tiara, almost; no wonder that the pirates had determined to give them a year to cool amidst the sands of the Bay of Whales.

"My!" said Tommie again, her eyes glittering as she gathered the things together carefully, spread the sack cloth and put them out.

She brooded on them without another word, picking them up one by one, trying the rings on, holding up the necklace for all to admire, even the Chinks, who had drawn close and who seemed to understand that these were the things for which they had been digging.

Then she put the lot on for fun, the tiara that nearly came over her ears, the necklace that nearly came down to her waist, the rings that hung loose on her fingers. Then, making a fan out of an old piece of paper, she got up and promenaded the sands, gathering up imaginary skirts and looking disdain upon her recent friends, till even the Chinks laughed.

Then, all at once, she quitted fooling, became preternaturally grave and, sitting down again, did the things up in the sack-cloth and oil skin.

George thought that she heaved a sigh as she tied the string. Hank noticed that she made a reef knot with her capable fingers and the fact gave him another little heart punch.

"They're worth a lot," said George.

"Thousands and thousands of dollars," said Tommie. "Here, take them and hide them somewhere safe."

Hank took the bundle. "I'm going to take them right aboard," declared he, "and shove them in the locker with the ship's money. I won't trust them another minute on this beach."

"Why, don't be a fool," said George, "we'll all be going aboard when Candon comes, we've done our work here."

"It's just on sundown," said Hank, "and if he's not here in another half hour, we'll have to stick the night. Can't get all these tents moved in the dark, and I'm not going to leave 'em. It's ten to one we'll stick till morning, and I'm not going to have those jewels stay the night with us. Something would happen sure. Maybe those greasers would come back with more men to help them."

"Not they. They won't stop running till next week."

"All the same these things have played us a good many tricks and I want to stop their game."

"Are you superstitious?" asked Tommie.

"Not a bit, only I've got a hunch that they're better on board."

"Oh, then, take them, take them," said George, "if you must. And see here, you'd better bring off those two automatics and some cartridges in case we don't get off to-night and those scamps make trouble."

"Sure," said Hank.

Off he started calling the Chinks to man the boat, whilst George and Tommie set to and began to build the fire.

Tommie, every now and then, took a glance towards the cliffs as though the absence of Candon were worrying her. When Hank came back he found them seated by the fire with the supper things spread, but no Candon.

"Hasn't B. C. come back?" asked Hank, sitting down.

"No," replied George.

The thought that he was still hunting for Tommie and that they had returned and were seated comfortably beginning their supper, came not only to the pair of them, but evidently, by her manner, to Miss Coulthurst. They tried to explain that they had come back not to give up the hunt, but to get the Chinks to help to comb the place, but the explanation seemed to fall rather flat.

"I hope to goodness nothing has happened to him," said George, weakly.

"Maybe you'd better go and see," suggested Tommie.

Hank jumped to his feet.

"Come on," he cried. George was scrambling up also when a hail came from towards the cliffs and they saw the figure of B. C. in the first of the starlight, coming towards them across the sands.

He spotted the figure of Tommie long before he reached them, and concluded that the others had found her and brought her back.

Walking like a man dead beat, he came up to them and cast himself down to rest on the sand.

"Thank God," said he.

"Where you been?" asked George.

"Been! Half over Mexico, kicking greasers, hunting—giv's a drink. Say—" to Tommie, "where did they find you?"

Tommie's only answer was a little squirt of laughter.

"She'd never gone," said Hank. Then he told the whole story.

Candon said nothing. Not one of them guessed the revolution that had suddenly taken place in his dead tired mind. Beyond the bald fact that he had made a fool of himself hunting for hours for something that was not there, stood the truth that fate had worked things so that whenever he moved towards a decent act he got a snub on the nose from somewhere. His attempt to return those jewels to their proper owners had brought the whole McGinnis crowd on top of him and had made him start on this mad expedition; his attempts to rescue Tommie from the white slavers had made him ridiculous, anyhow to himself; this wild search of the last few hours had made him ridiculous in the eyes of his companions.

One thing called up another till the hell broth in his mind, the feeling of "damn, everything" was almost complete. What completed it was Tommie's spurt of laughter. That was fatal.

He said nothing but began eating his supper with the rest. Then Hank, suddenly remembering the jewels, broke out, "Say! I forgot, we've got a surprise for you. I'll give you a hundred guesses and I'll bet you won't tell what it is."

"It's the boodle," cut in George.

Then they told.

Candon showed neither pleasure nor surprise, he went on eating.

"Well, where is it?" said he at last.

"On the yacht," said Hank. "I rowed over and stowed it away, just before you came."

"You rowed over and stowed it away. What did you do that for?"

"Safety."

"Safety—did you expect I was going to steal it?"

"Lord! B. C.," said Hank, "what's getting at you?"

"Nothing," said Candon, suddenly blazing out: "Well, as you have taken the stuff on board, you can take it back to 'Frisco without me. The expedition's ended. You start off back to-morrow, I stay here. I've fulfilled my part of the contract. I've brought Vanderdecken on board your ship and I've brought you to the stuff and you've got it. In the contract I was to receive so much money down. I don't want it. I can hoof it down to Mazatlan and get work among the Mexicans. You can leave me one of the automatics and some cartridges, that's all I want."

George sat aghast; so did Hank.

It was as if B. C. had turned inside out before their eyes.

"Look here," said George at last, "that's nonsense. We are all good friends. Vanderdecken has nothing to do with us or that boodle. Good Lord! What's come to you?"

"It's come to me that I'm sick of the show," said B. C. "I've done my part, the expedition is over as far as I'm concerned and I stay here. You'll be leaving early in the morning?"

"Sun-up," said Hank.

"Well, you can leave a couple of days' grub for me and one of the automatics in case I have any trouble with these fellows. That's all, but I'll see you in the morning before you start."

They saw he was in earnest and in no temper for discussion, neither of them spoke.

Then Candon, having finished, got up and walked down to the beach.

Tommie had not said a word.

George was the first to speak.

"What ails him, what in the nation's got into his head?"

"Search me," said Hank, in a dreary voice, "unless it's this expedition. I was saying before he came back there was something wrong with it, has been from the start. I dunno—well, here we are, and how are we to leave him without money or anything? Why, I've got as fond of that lad as if he was my own brother and he turns like that on us."

"Maybe he's tired," said Tommie, "and if you talk to him in the morning, you'll find him different."

"I don't believe it," said George, "he means what he says. Question is, what's turned him on us?"

"Turned him on us? Why, my taking those rotten diamonds off to the ship—what else? I didn't know he'd take it like that, how could I?"

"Then go and explain," said George, "go and tell him you're sorry."

"Me! what's there to be sorry for?"

"Well, it was a fool's game, anyhow."

"Which?"

"Carting that stuff off on board."

"We ain't all as clever as you, I know," said Hank. "S'pose those Mexicans come down to-night on us, you'll see if it was a fool's game getting the valuables off first. I tell you we ought to have cleared off this evening, it's plain not safe sticking here the night. We *would* have cleared only for B. C., fooling about."

"He was looking for me," quietly put in Tommie.

Hank, squashed for the moment, was silent, then he said: "Well, maybe, but there we are, in about as dangerous a fix as people could be, and you talk of fools' games."

"By the way," said George, "have you brought off those automatics?"

"Those which—automatics—Lord, no—I forgot, clean. How's a chap to be remembering things, running backwards and forwards from that damned ship? Clean——"

"Well, it's not the first thing you've forgotten, and if you're so anxious about the Mexicans, you'd better go and fetch them."

"Me! I ain't going to fetch and carry any more. Go yourself."

"Pistols aren't any use," said Tommie, suddenly as if awaking from a reverie. "If those people come, there'll be so many of them it won't be any use firing at them and if any of them were shot, we might get into trouble."

"Seems to me we're mighty near it."

"Mighty near which?" asked a voice.

Candon had returned and was standing just outside the fire zone. He seemed in a slightly better temper.

"Why, Hank here has forgot to bring off the automatics," said George, "and he's afraid of those Mexicans coming down on us in the night."

"Lord, I hadn't thought of that," said B. C. almost in his old voice. "Well, I'll go off and fetch them. I've got to fetch a couple of things I've left in my locker anyway." He turned.

"Fetch the ammunition if you're going," said George.

"Sure."

They heard him calling the Chinks, then the boat put off.

"Seems he's still bent on quitting," said Hank.

George yawned.

If the air of the Bay of Whales could be condensed and bottled, morphia would be a drug in the drug market. It had the two men now firmly in its grip. They determined to turn in without waiting for B. C., and Tommie, retiring to her tent, seemed as heavy with sleep as the others. She was not. She did not undress but just lay down on a blanket, her chin in the palms of her hands and gazing out on the starlit beach as though hypnotized.

She was gazing at Candon.

He was the only man she had ever thought twice about, he was different from the others, she could not tell how. The fact that he was Vanderdecken did not make this difference, nor the fact that he had picked her up and literally run away with her, nor the fact that he had beautiful blue eyes. He was just different and she felt that she would never meet anyone like him again.

Yet he was going to leave them. Instinctively she knew why. That outburst when they found the cache sanded over gave her some knowledge of his temperament; and the fact that he had almost killed himself hunting for her gave her some hint of his care for her. And she had laughed at him.

She remembered how he had said: "Thank God!" on finding her safe.

She rose and came out of the tent on to the sands. She had come to the determination that if he stayed behind here on the morrow, it would not be her fault, and, coming down to the sea edge, she sat down on the beach to wait for the returning boat.

The sound of the waves on the long beach came mixed with the breath of the sea. The reefs spoke sometimes and the wind, blowing from the north-west, stirred the sand with a silken whispering sound that would die off to nothing and then return.

Sometimes she fancied that she could hear the creak of oars, and, rising, strained her eyes to catch a glimpse of the coming boat. Nothing. She could not see the anchor light of the *Wear Jack* owing to the faint sea haze, and taking her seat again on the sands, she resumed her watch whilst the time passed and the stars moved and the tide went further out.

Then she rose. Candon was evidently remaining for the night on the *Wear Jack*; there was no use in waiting longer. Still she waited, standing and looking out to sea.

At last, she turned and came back to the tents.

She would see him in the morning, but the others would be there. It would be quite different then. The moment had passed and gone, and would not return.

Arrived at her tent, she undressed and got into her pyjamas and crawled under a blanket which she pulled over her head. Then, safely hidden, and with her face in the crook of her arm, she sniveled and sobbed, remembered she had not said her prayers and said them, sniffed some more and fell asleep. Poor Tommie. She did not know what she wanted but she knew she wanted it. She felt she had lost something but she did not know it was her heart.

CHAPTER XXXIII

GONE!

THE sun got up and struck the hills of Sinaloa, the plains of sagebrush, rock and sand, the sea.

The Bay of Whales, lit from end to end and shouting with gulls, faced an ocean destitute of sign of ship or sail.

George awoke in the tent and gazed for a moment lazily at the honey-coloured patch on the sail cloth above his head, where the sun was laying a finger. He heard the waves on the beach and the crying of the gulls, the wind through the tent-opening came fresh and pure, and he knew it was good to be alive. Alive in a clean world where the wind was a person and the sun the chief character after God's earth and sea. Then Candon came blowing into his mind and he remembered the incidents of the night before and how B. C. had gone off the handle over something, he could not guess what, and how he had planned to leave them that day. All this he remembered in the first few seconds of waking—and then he recognised that Candon was not in the tent and that his blankets were carefully rolled up and stowed for the day. He must have got up early and gone out; probably he was building the fire.

He gave the sleeping Hank a dig, and woke him up.

"Hank," said George.

"Yep?"

"I've been thinking of B. C."

"What's the matter with B. C.?"

"Wake up, you old mud turtle. He's leaving us to-day and we've just got not to let him go."

"Oh, ay," said Hank, remembering things. Then he yawned frightfully, blinked and looked around.

"Where's he gone?"

"He's got up early—outside somewhere. Say, we've got to keep him—have a straight talk with him. He's one of the best for all his queer ways."

"Sure," said Hank.

Fully awake now, he rose and slipped into his clothes, George following suit. Hank was the first out. He stepped on to the sand, looked round for Candon and then looked out to sea.

"*Jumping* Moses!"

"What's wrong?" cried George, coming out. "What are you——Good *gosh*!" He had followed the pointing of Hank's finger. The *Wear Jack* was gone.

Almost at the same moment came Tommie's voice from her tent door. "Why, where's the ship?"

"Gone," said Hank. "Drifted—sunk—but what in the nation could have sunk her? How could she have drifted? Oh, hell! It can't be that B. C. has bolted with her—say—Bud——"

"It is," said George, "bolted with her and the boodle. We've been stung—that's all."

"I don't believe it," said Tommie. Her little face looked like a piece of chalk and she was holding on to the tent flap.

"There you are," said Hank. "Nor I. B. C. couldn't do it, that's all. He couldn't do it."

"He's done it," said George. "He was sore about your taking the stuff off to the ship because he intended bunking with it himself—can't you see?"

"Maybe those Chinks have taken the ship," said Hank.

George shook his head. "We'd have heard him shout with the wind blowing that way. Besides, they couldn't. Not one of them has any notion of navigating her. Can't you see? He's got the boodle. He's meant to do this all along when the stuff turned up and he's done it."

"I tell you that chap's a white man," began Hank, furiously.

"In spots," said George, "or in streaks—as he said himself. He runs straight for a while, *wants* to run straight and then goes off the other way about. He's a socialist, grand ideas and a slung shot in his pocket."

"Socialist, so'm I."

"No you're not, you're Hank Fisher."

Hank went off a few yards and sat down on the sand and folded his arms and brooded. His good soul had been hit and hit hard. Even while defending Candon, he recognised the logic of the situation, pointing to the almost unbelievable fact that Candon, yielding to his worst nature, had bolted. Bolted, leaving them stranded on that beach.

He could not but recognise that for a man in Candon's position, leaving morality aside, the move was a good one. His return to San Francisco was impossible, McGinnis would merely turn evidence against him. Leaving the Vanderdecken business aside, there was the wrecking of the junk; the *Wear Jack* herself was attainted. All sorts of new ideas began to turn somersaults in Hank's mind as this fact burst fully for the first time on his intelligence.

"Bud," he shouted, "come here and sit. Where's T. C.? Call her. Sit down."

They came and sat down.

"Folks," said Hank, "here's a new tangle. Hasn't it ever struck into you that the old *Jack's* n'more use to us than an opera hat to a bull. Those movie men don't know her name, but they know her make and that she went south, see? And every yacht coming up from the south anythink like her will be overhauled by the coastguard, see? Well, suppose we'd put back in her, getting along for the Islands, the coastguard would have been sure to board us, they'd have found T. C. aboard and we'd have been dished, straight."

"I hadn't thought it out like that before," said George. "I thought we could have slipped up to 'Frisco and then told some yarn."

Tommie said nothing. The colour had almost returned to her face, but she seemed like a person slightly dazed. No wonder. Despite, or maybe partly because of his confession to her, partly because of his evident care for her and partly because of her newborn affection for him, she would have trusted B. C. with anything, her life, her money, anything—this man who had betrayed her, betrayed Bud and Hank, taken their ship and left them stranded on a hostile beach.

"Well, we couldn't," said Hank. "The fact is the *Wear Jack* was no use to us and maybe it was Providence that made B. C. let us down."

"Maybe," said Tommie, catching at straws, "she drifted away."

"That's what I thought first," said George, "but she couldn't. She was anchored fast. If she had, why she could have put back. What's the good of supposing, when the thing's clear as paint. He was boss of the ship, the Chinks always looked to him for orders, they'd do whatever he told them, and when he went aboard last night and told them to knock off the shackles and drop the anchor chain, they wouldn't grumble. If they thought anything, they'd think it was part of some move in the game and we were in it. We've made several big mistakes, but the biggest was letting that guy be boss."

"Well, he was boss, anyhow," said the ingenuous Hank. "He was the best man of us three in the practical business and I'm not saying he wasn't the best in brains. He couldn't run straight, that's all; if he could he might have been President by this."

They all sat silent for a minute, then George sprang to his feet.

"Breakfast," said George.

Not another word was spoken of Candon. It was as though he had been expelled from their minds as from their society.

But they could not expel the situation he had created. Though the *Wear Jack* was no use for taking them back to San Francisco, it could have taken them somewhere—anywhere from that beach where the fume of the sea and the sun and the silence and desolation and the blinding sands and mournful cliffs had already begun to tell upon them now that the place was a prison. Then there were the Mexicans to be thought of. If those men whom they had kicked and man-handled and robbed of their booty were to return with a dozen others, what would happen? How could two men and a girl put up any sort of fight? And the dreadful thing was Tommie. Tommie, who had stuck to them because she was a brick, who, to save them from a ridicule almost as bad as disgrace, had insisted on going on. If she had turned back, she might have been safe at Los Angeles now instead of here. This thought hit Bud almost as badly as Hank.

It did not seem to hit Tommie at all. There were moments during the preparation of breakfast when the throat muscles of the redoubtable T. C. made movements as though she were swallowing down the recollection of Candon, but, the meal once begun, she seemed herself again.

As they ate, they discussed the situation in all its bearings. They had provisions enough for three weeks, according to Hank's calculations. He suggested that they should hang on just there for a day or two, and then, if nothing turned up in the way of a ship, that they should "hike" down the coast towards the town "that fellow" had spoken of.

"What was the name of it?" asked George.

"Search me," replied Hank, "but it don't matter, the name, it's a town anyhow."

"And suppose, while we're hanging on here, those Mexicans come at us?" asked George.

Hank had forgotten the Mexicans.

"If they do," said he, "we'll have to fight them, that's all. We've got the spades, and two Americans are a match for a dozen greasers, and there's not likely to be that number."

George got up and walked off down to the sea edge. He seemed to be thinking things over.

Hank found himself alone with Tommie.

"You meant three Americans," said she.

"Sure," said Hank, "you'd put up as good a fight as any of us, I believe."

Hank had never dealt much with women-kind, except maybe in that horrible business liaison of his with Mrs. Driscoll, and though he had read the "Poems of Passion" by Ella Wheeler Wilcox he had no language at all to garb his sentiments with, if you can dignify with the title of sentiment a desire to eat Tommie.

He heaved a deep sigh and began tracing patterns on the sand with his finger. The rat trap inventor was at fault, his ingenuity could not assist him, the civilized man who believed in the sanctity of womanhood and the primitive man who wanted to make a meal of T. C. were at war, but the primitive man was the stronger and was preparing to speak and make a fool of himself when a yell came from George.

"Ship!"

They sprang to their feet and came running to the water's edge. They could see nothing; then, following his pointing, away on the sea line, they saw what looked like the wing of a fly.

"It's the *Wear Jack*," said Hank, "no, it ain't—her canvas wouldn't show as dark as that."

"How's she bearing?" asked George.

"Coming right in, I believe. She's got the wind with her; that's her fore canvas. There'd be more spread if she was sideways to us or tacking against the wind. Yes, she's coming right for us."

"Good," said George.

There was silence for a moment, a silence more indicative than any words could be of the relief that had come to their minds. It was suddenly shattered by Hank.

"She's the *Heart of Ireland*."

"What you say?" cried George.

"She's the *Heart of Ireland*."

"How do you know?"

"Lord! how do I know? I know. I feel it. What else can she be? Why she's *due*. She's just had time to mend herself and put out. What other boat would be putting into this God-forsaken place? And she seems about the size of the *Heart*. We'll soon see. I've got the specification down in my head, that fellow gave it to me—two topmast, fifty-ton schooner, broad beam and dirty as Hades. Those are her beauty marks—we'll soon see."

"But she'd have passed the *Wear Jack*," said George.

"Not if the *Jack* went south. And anyhow they'd have passed in the night; wouldn't have seen each other."

"What are we to do?" asked Tommie.

"I'm thinking," said Hank. He looked round, brooded for a moment, and then stood looking out to sea. His ingenuity was at work. Then he spoke.

"There are no caves in these cliffs or we might hide there. No use scattering inland. First of all, if these chaps find nothing but the tents they'll think us gone and they'll go off with the tents and grub and everything. Then where would we be? We've got to hide and watch for chances."

"Where?" asked George.

Hank pointed to the big rock before-mentioned, shaped like a pulpit, that stood close to them by the sea edge.

"There, standing close up to it, we can dodge them when they're coming ashore. Then when they land we can shift round to the north side of it, see?"

"I see," said George, "but where's the use? Suppose we manage to hide entirely from them, where's the use? They'll take the tents and stores as you said—and where will we be?"

"Now see here," said the rat trap man. "It's ten to one the whole crowd will come ashore, leaving only a couple of guys to look after the ship. They'll beach the boat, leaving a man to look after her and scatter up to the tents, see?"

"Yes."

"Well, there's a chance that we may be able to make a dash for the boat, knock the chap on the head, push her off and get to the schooner."

"Good!" cried Tommie.

"And suppose there's a lot of fellows on the schooner?" asked George.

"Oh, suppose anything. What do you think this show is? If I know anything of that crowd, it's our lives we are playing for and the chances are a hundred to one against us. It all depends where they beach the boat. Come along, it's time to get to eastward of that rock."

Hank, picking up a water beaker and a cup, they moved off to the rock and put it between them and the sea.

Before taking shelter, Hank shaded his eyes and looked out to sea.

"It'll take them near an hour to get in," said he.

Half an hour passed and then the thirst began. Used as they were to the sun, they had never before experienced the ordeal of sitting still with the sun's rays beating on them. Fortunately they wore panamas and the wind from the sea licked round the rock every little while, bringing a trace of coolness. Hank poured out the water and they drank in turn every now and then. He insisted on wetting Tommie's head occasionally. They talked in whispers and scarcely at all, listening—listening—listening. Time passed, bringing gulls' voices, the beat of the little waves on the beach, the silky whisper of the sand, then suddenly far away—

Rumble-tumble-tum-tum-tum.

The sound of an anchor chain running through a hawse pipe.

They looked at one another.

"That's the killick," murmured Hank. "It's them right enough, they've come right in knowing the ground, they wouldn't have been in so quick if they hadn't been used to the place. Listen!" He had no need to tell them to listen.

Time passed and the beach talked but no sound came from the sea but the sound of the small waves.

Tommie suddenly nudged Hank. She nodded towards the cliffs. On the sky edge of the cliffs something black showed, then it withdrew.

"Men," whispered Tommie.

"Mexicans," murmured Hank. The eerie feeling came to him that behind those cliffs, in the gullies, men were swarming: that Sinaloa had beaten up its bandits and desperadoes, just as he had expected it would, and that the call of the diamonds like the call of a corpse in the desert was bringing the vultures. They would connect this new crowd just about to land with the treasure business. If they showed themselves too soon, then McGinnis and his men would be frightened off. McGinnis was bad, but the Mexicans were worse. Hank did not often say his prayers, but he prayed just then that cunning might be granted to the greasers not to shout before the game was corralled.

He needn't.

There came far away voices from the sea and the creak of oars—nearer.

"Get your hind legs ready," whispered Hank.

Crash! the oars were in. Then came a burst of yells as though a pack of demons had suddenly been unleashed and unmuzzled.

Hank sprang to his feet. Leading the others, he dodged round the north side to the seaward side of the rock. A hundred and fifty yards away to the south a big boat had been beached. It lay unattended. Like a pack of hounds on a hot scent the McGinnis crowd were racing up towards the tents. You could have covered them with a blanket. Blind to everything but loot and vengeance, a trumpet would not have turned them.

Hank seized Tommie by the hand and started.

It was a hundred and fifty yards from the rock to the boat, the going good over a strip of hard sand uncovered by the ebbing tide.

From the boat to the nearest tent was about a hundred yards, the going bad over soft friable sand.

They had made fifty yards unnoticed, when Tommie tripped and fell. Hank picked her up and flung her on his shoulder.

The ruffians, racing from tent to tent hunting, cursing, rooting about, saw nothing till Pat McGinnis himself, turning from Tommie's tent empty like the rest, saw the whole of Hank's cards on the table—so to speak.

All but the ace of trumps.

He whipped it from his belt, aimed, took a long shot on chance, and, leading the others, raced back for the sea edge.

CHAPTER XXXIV

JAKE

HANK had dropped Tommie into the boat and was striving with George to push off, when the crack of the revolver came followed by the bizz of the bullet, yards out.

"Shove her—shove her," cried Hank. The huge brute of a scow had settled herself comfortably in the sand as if she meant to take up her residence there. Tommie, tumbling out of the boat nearly as quickly as she had been thrown in, put her shoulder to the stem; Hank and George at either gunnel clutched hard. Hank gave the word and they all heaved together. Next moment they were on board her and she was water-borne.

Hank seized one of the ash sweeps and using it as a pole drove her half a dozen yards, she slued round sideways, but George in the bow had a sweep out now and with a stroke pulled her nose round whilst Hank took his seat.

As they got away on her, McGinnis, leading the hunt, was only twenty yards from the sea. He was holding his fire, as were the others, till they reached the water's edge, when the bang of an old musket that might have landed with Padre Junipero made the echoes jump alive.

The attackers wheeled.

Down through the two defiles and fanning out on the sands, pouring like ants, came the countryside for all it was worth, half a hundred beggars and landed proprietors, zambos and terzerons, yellow men and men who were almost black, armed with anything and everything and led by the "Dredging Machine." A fellow who had tumbled in his hurry was picking himself up. It was his musket that had gone off by accident.

"Pull!" shouted Hank.

They were saved. The McGinnis crowd, like a pack of wild dogs chased by wolves, were racing along the water edge towards the south horn of the bay; the Mexicans, faced by the facts of the sand and a proposition in Euclid, had paused for half a moment. The direct line towards the south horn of the bay was hard going over the soft sand, but it was shorter than making direct for the hard beach. Two sides of a triangle being longer than the third, they took the shorter way.

The rowers as they rowed watched the race, and saw plainly that McGinnis and his merry men were making good. Then they turned their attention to the ship ahead. She was swinging to the current broadside on to them, a frowsy looking two-topmast schooner, the *Heart of Ireland* sure enough.

"Wonder how many chaps are on board," said George.

"We'll soon see," replied Hank.

As they drew closer they saw a man leaning on the rail and watching them through a pair of binoculars. He seemed the only person on the ship.

Closer now, the old schooner began to speak of her disreputability. The paint, in Hank's words, was less paint than blisters, the canvas, hurriedly stowed, was discoloured and patched—old stuff re-done by the hand of McGay, that stand-by of small ship owners in these days when a new mainsail for a small boat costs anything from two hundred dollars. Built in 1882 as a trading schooner, she had been built a bit too small, but she had looked honest when the fitters and riggers had done with her; honest, clean and homely, in those first days one might have compared her to a country girl starting for market with a basket a bit too small.

In two years this simple trader had changed her vocation; in thirty-five years she had done pretty much everything that a ship ought not to do, run guns, run gin and opium, fished in prohibited waters, and in some extraordinary way she bore the stamp of it all. If some ship lover had seen the *Mary Burton*—that was her first name—and the *Heart of Ireland*, which was her last, he might have been excused, if a moral man, for weeping.

"Ahoy!" cried Hank, as the boat came alongside grinding the blisters off her. "Fling's a rope there—why! Good Lord! It's Jake."

It was. Jake, looking just the same as when Hank had fired him off the *Wear Jack*, only now, instead of a fur cap, he was wearing a dingy white Stetson with the brim turned down. He had come along with the McGinnis crowd, partly because he wanted a job and partly because he wanted to see the downfall of Hank. As a matter of fact he had seen the triumph of Hank, if you can call it a triumph, for he had been watching the whole of the proceedings from start to finish. Recognising the inevitable he made no bones but flung the rope.

"Well, you scoundrel," said Hank, as he came on deck, "what you doing here?"

"What you doin' yourself?" said Jake.

"I'll jolly soon show you," said Hank, who had no time to waste in verbal explanations. Seizing the scamp by the shoulders, he turned him round in some extraordinary way and giving him a shove that sent him running forward two yards. "Get the gaskets off the jib and look slippy about it—

quick now or I'll be after you. Bud, I'm going to leave the boat. There's a dinghy aboard and that scow would clutter up the decks too much. Cut her adrift and come on. Clap on to the throat an' peak halyards, now then, all together, yeo ho!"

Mainsail and foresail took the wind at last. And what a mainsail it was, after the canvas of the *Wear Jack*, dirty as a dishcloth and patched where a pilot mark had once been. And what sticks after the spars of the *Jack*, from the main boom, that had seen better days, to the gaff, with its wooden jaws bound to creak like a four-post bedstead!

"Now the winch," cried Hank. "Clap on to the winch and roust her out."

He took the wheel, whilst Jake, Tommie and Bud clapped on to the winch, and, as he stood listening to the music of the chain coming in, he cast his eyes away towards the south horn of the bay where the McGinnis crew could be seen moving slowly now towards the bay beyond, followed by the Mexicans, evidently half-beaten, but still doggedly in pursuit.

"She's out of the mud!" cried George.

Hank turned the spokes of the wheel, and the *Heart*, with all her canvas thrashing, took the wind, got steerage way on her, and, as the anchor came home, lay over on the starboard tack.

She had been anchored to north of the break in the reefs and this course would take her diagonally through the break.

Hank, who had bitten off a piece of plug tobacco, stood, working his lantern jaws as he steered. Gulls raced them as they went and the breeze strengthened up, whilst block, spar and cordage creaked to the boost of the waves and the slap of the bow wash. They passed the horn of the northern reef by a short ten yards, the out-going tide and the south-running current foaming round the rocks like destruction gnashing at them. Then, lifting her bowsprit, the *Heart* took the great sea, dipping and rising again to the steadily marching swell.

Hank held on. The wind was breezing up strong from the southwest and he was keeping her close hauled. A few miles out, with Mexico a cloud on the sea line and the reefs a memory, he spun the wheel and laid her on a due westerly course.

He called Jake.

"You can steer?"

"Sure," said Jake.

"Then catch hold and keep her as she is." He stood watching whilst Jake steered.

That individual, despite the shove he had received, seemed to bear no malice. Absolutely unperturbed he stood with his hands on the spokes, chewing, his eye wandering from the binnacle to the luff of the mainsail.

"Whar's the *Jack*?" he suddenly asked, turning to spit into the starboard scupper.

"What were you doing with that gang?" countered Hank.

"Me! Them guys? Why, you saw what I was doin', keepin' ship, whiles they went ashore. What were *you* doin' with them?"

"Mean to tell me you don't know why they went ashore?"

"Me! nuthin'. I'm only a foremast hand, signed on 'cause I was out of a job. I saw you all scatterin' about on shore, then you comes off and takes the ship—that's all I know."

"Look here," said Hank. "D'you mean to tell me you didn't put the McGinnis crowd on to us before we left 'Frisco? D'you mean to say you weren't on the wharf that night when Black Mullins dropped aboard and peeked through the skylight and saw Mr. Candon?"

"Me. Which? Me! N'more than Adam. You're talkin' French."

"Don't bother with him," said George. "Come on down below and let's see what it's like."

They left the deck to Jake, still chewing, and came down the companion way to the cabin, where McGinnis and his afterguard had dwelt.

Bunks with tossed blankets appeared on either side; aft lay the captain's cabin, door open and an oilskin swinging like a corpse from a nail; above, and through the atmosphere of must and bad tobacco, came the smell of the *Heart*, a perfume of shark oil, ineradicable, faint, but unforgettable, once smelt.

George opened the portholes and Tommie took her seat on a bunk edge, looking round her but saying nothing.

A cheap brass lamp swung from the beam above the table, the table was covered with white marbled oilcloth, stained and stamped with innumerable ring marks from the bottoms of coffee cups; about the whole place was that atmosphere of sordidness and misery that man alone can create.

Tommie sat absorbing it, whilst Hank and George explored lockers and investigated McGinnis' cabin. Then she rose and took off her coat.

She stripped the oilcloth from the table, said, "Faugh!" rolled it up and flung it on the floor.

"Say!" cried she, "isn't there any soap in this hooker?"

"Soap!" cried Hank, appearing from McGinnis' cabin, carrying the log book and a tin box. "I dunno. Jake will know."

"Go up and send him down. You can take the wheel for a minute whilst I get this place clean—Goodness!"

"You wait," said Hank.

He went on deck, followed by George, and next minute Jake appeared.

Despite Tommie's get-up, he had spotted her for a girl when she came on board. Not being a haunter of the pictures he had not recognised her; what she was, or where she had come from, he could not imagine—or what she wanted of him. He was soon to learn.

"Take off your hat," said Tommie. "Now, then, get me some soap and a scrubbing brush, if there is such a thing on this dirty ship."

"Soap!" said Jake.

"Yes, soap."

He turned and went on deck and came back in a minute or so with a tin of soft soap and a mop.

"I said scrubbing brush."

"Ain't none."

"Well, we'll have to make the mop do. Now go and fetch a bucket of water."

"Ain't enough on board for swillin'."

"There's enough in the sea. We must make it do. Go on and don't stand there scratching your head."

Hank, leaving George at the wheel and coming down half an hour later to see what was going on, returned jubilant.

"She's working that gink like a house maid, he's washed the table an's scrubbing the floor and she's stripping the blankets off the bunks. She's going to make him wash them. She's a peach."

The tin box with the ship's money, some thousand dollars, and the log lay on the deck. He placed them on one side and then stood erect and walked to the rail. He gazed aft at the far-away shore as if visualising something there.

"Bud."

"Yep?"

"Nothing's ever got me like she has, right by the neck. I reckon it's a punishment on me for having invented rat traps."

"Oh, don't be an ass."

"Easy to say that."

"Have you told her?"

"Lord, no."

"Well, go down and tell her and get it over, same as sea sickness."

"Bud, I could no more tell her than I could walk into a blazing fiery furnace like those chaps in the Scriptures."

"Why?"

"Because, Bud—well, there's two reasons. First of all she'd laugh at me, maybe."

"She would, sure."

"And then—there's a girl—"

"Yes."

"A girl—another girl."

"Mrs. Driscoll?"

"Oh. Lord, no, she ain't a girl. This one I'm telling you of is running a little store of her own in Cable Street, kind of fancy work business—I've known her a year. O'Brien is her name, Zillah O'Brien. She's running a fancy work—"

"I know, you've told me; are you engaged to her?"

"Well, we've been keeping company," said Hank, "and it amounts to that."

"You mean you are—then you've no right to bother about Tommie."

"It's she that's bothering me."

"Well, you may make your mind easy. So far as I can see she's harpooned—that fellow harpooned her."

"B. C.?"

"Yep, remember her face when he ran away? And ever since she hasn't been the same—"

Hank was silent for a moment.

"But, Bud, she couldn't care for him after the way he's landed us?"

"No, but she cared for him before, and maybe she cares for him still, Lord only knows—women are funny things. Anyhow, you've no right to think of her with that other girl in tow. Why, Hank, you've always been going on about women being saints and all that and now, you old double-dealing—"

"It isn't me," said Hank. "I guess it's human nature. But I'll bite on the bullet—after all it's not so much as a girl I care for her, but just for herself."

"Well, bite on what's her name as well—Beliah—"

"Zillah."

"All the same, keep thinking of her—and catch hold of the wheel. I want a quiet smoke."

Half an hour later Jake wandered on deck with the mop and the bucket. He look subdued, and a few minutes later Tommie's head and shoulders appeared.

"The place is pretty clean now," said T. C. "Maybe some of you will get at where the food's stowed and find out what we can have to eat. I'm going along to the galley to get the fire on."

CHAPTER XXXV

SANTANDER ROCK

THE wind held steady all that day and half the following night, then it died to a tepid breeze just sufficient to keep steerage way on the schooner.

Hank was the first up in the morning, relieving George at the wheel.

After supper, on the night before, they had made a plan, based on the fact that there were provisions on board enough for a three months' cruise for four people. This plan was simple enough. They would put out far to avoid the Islands and any bother of complications. Hank's idea was to strike a course nor'west to a point midway between Honolulu and San Francisco, and then make directly for the city of the Golden Gate. They would tell Tyrebuck the truth, but it would be no sin to delude the gaping public with a Hank constructed yarn, sure that McGinnis or his relations would never dispute it. The only bother was that Tyrebuck would want his ten thousand dollars. If the *Wear Jack* had been wrecked, all would have been well, for the insurance people would have paid, but they had just lost her, as a person might lose a horse or a motor car.

"Of course," said Hank, "there was no agreement with him. Who'd have ever imagined such a thing as our losing her like that? All the same, I've got to pay old man Tyrebuck, it's a debt of honour. I'll have to mortgage the trap that's all."

"I'll go half," said George.

"No, you won't. I was the borrower, this expedition was mine. If I'd got the twenty-five thousand reward, I'd have stuck to it."

"Say," said George.

"Yep."

"You told me you'd written a story once."

"What about it?"

"Well, write the whole of this expedition up and sell it to a magazine, if you want money."

"B'gosh!" said Hank, "that's not a bad idea—only it would give the show away."

"Not a bit, pretend it's fiction."

"It sounds like fiction," said Tommie. "I don't mind. You can stick me in as much as you like."

"I'll do it, maybe," said Hank.

But there was another point. Wallack's and their wrecked junk, and Tommie and her story. The public would want to know the particulars of her abduction and Wallack's would want compensation. Althusen and Moscovitch and Mrs. Raphael would not be behindhand in their wants, either.

"Leave it to me," said Miss Coulthurst. "When we get to San Francisco, just let me slip on shore, and I'll take the first train to Los Angeles and I'll fix it. I'll tell old Wallack the whole truth. He won't want compensation. I guess the advertisement he's had will be enough for him, and the film wasn't damaged; the reel was safe in one of those tents."

They left it at that, ignorant of the new development impending.

Hank took the wheel and George snuffed out the binnacle lights. It was day, though the sun had not yet broken the morning bank on the eastern horizon.

"There's a big rock on the port bow," said George, "away over there. It's the Santander, I believe—remember? It's on the chart."

"Where's Jake?"

"Right," said Hank. "Where's Jake? I let him turn in ten minutes ago, he's in the focs'le."

"Well, I'll go and make some coffee," said George. "Keep her as she goes."

He disappeared, and Hank, left alone, stood at the wheel, the warm wind gently lifting his hair and his hawk eyes wandering from the binnacle to the far off rock and from the rock to the sea line.

Ten minutes passed and then George appeared, a cup of coffee in his hand.

"Shove her on the deck for a minute," said Hank, "and have a look with those binoculars. Something funny about that rock, seems to me."

George placed the cup on the deck, fetched the old binoculars Jake had been using the day before, and leveled them at the rock.

"Ship piled on the north side," said George. "I can see the masts; some sort of small hooker or another. It's the Santander rock, can't be anything else, there's nothing else of any size marked down just here but the Tres Marias Island, and they are to the south."

"Well, we'll have a look at her," said Hank. "There's maybe some poor devils on board. She's flying no signals, is she?"

"No, she's signal enough in herself."

Just then Tommie came on deck.

She had a look through the binoculars and then went off to the galley with George to see about breakfast. There were plenty of provisions on the *Heart*; McGinnis and his crew had evidently plenty of cash or credit, to judge by the condition of the lazarette and store room, and when Tommie and George had satisfied their wants, Hank, giving them the deck, came down.

When he returned on deck, the schooner was closing up with the rock and the wreck was plainly visible to the naked eye, with the gulls shouting around her.

The Santander rock, shaped and spired like a cathedral, runs north and south, three hundred yards long, two hundred feet high, caved here and there by the sea and worn by wind and rain into ledges and depressions where the gulls roost—where they have roosted for ten thousand years.

It is the top of a big submarine mountain that rises gradually from the depth of a mile. Quite in shore, on the northern side, the lead gives a depth of only twenty fathoms, gradually deepening, as you put away, by five fathoms to the hundred yards, till suddenly the lead finds nothing. There must be a sheer, unimaginable cliff just there, some three quarters of a mile high!

It was on the north side of this great rock, which is at once a monstrous and a tragic figure, that the wreck was skewered, listing to starboard, her sticks still standing but her canvas unstowed. The crew had evidently piled her there, perhaps in the dark.

Now, drawing close to her, that stern seemed familiar, and the fact that she was a yacht became apparent. It was Hank who voiced the growing conviction in their minds.

"Boys!" cried Hank, "she's the *Wear Jack*!"

George and Tommie were the only boys on that deck beside himself, but Tommie did not laugh. She heaved a deep breath and stood with her hands on the rail and her eyes fixed on the wreck.

"She is," said George. "Look at her paint. Lord, this is lovely, that fellow has piled her."

"And got off in the boat," said Hank. "The boat's gone. They'd have easy lowered her over the starboard side."

"What are you going to do?" asked the other. "Shall we board her?"

"Sure," said Hank. "Roust out Jake and get ready to drop the hook if we can find anchorage. Get the lead ready."

George ran to the foc's'le and rousted out Jake who came on deck rubbing his eyes.

"Why there's the—old *Jack*," cried he. "Piled!" He clapped his hand on his thigh, then fetched the lead at the order of Hank and hove it.

Forty fathoms rocky bottom, was the result. Then, as they came slowly up, the depth shoaled.

"Get ready with the anchor," cried Hank. He brought the *Heart* along till they were almost abreast of the wreck, and at a safe distance, then, in thirty fathoms, the anchor was dropped and the *Heart* slowly swung to her moorings.

The dinghy was lowered and Hank and George got in.

Yes, it was the *Wear Jack* right enough, lying there like a stricken thing, the gentle list bringing her starboard rail to within a few feet of the blue lapping swell. Gaffs brought down on the booms, booms unsupported by the topping lifts, boat gone, she made a picture of desolation and abandonment unforgettable, seen there against the grim gray background of the rock.

"Well, he's made a masterpiece of it," said Hank as they tied on and scrambled on board. "He sure has."

They were turning aft along the slanting deck when up through the cabin hatch came the head and shoulders of a man, a man rubbing sleep from his eyes. It was Candon.

CHAPTER XXXVI

"CANDON"

CANDON—deserted by the Chinks just as he had deserted his companions on the beach.

"It's him—the scoundrel," cried Hank.

Candon, as startled as themselves, wild-eyed and just roused from profound sleep, standing now on deck staring at Hank, took the insult right in his teeth.

He drew back a bit, glanced over, saw the *Heart* and turned to George.

"What's this?" said Candon. "Where the hell have you come from?"

"Where you left us stranded on that beach," replied George. "Where you left us when you beat it with the ship and the boodle."

Candon's face blazed up for a second. Then he got a clutch on himself and seemed to bottle his pride and his anger. He folded his arms and stared at the deck planking without speaking. He rocked slightly as he stood, as though unsure of his balance. He seemed to have no sense of shame. Caught and confronted with his deed, he did not seem even to be searching for excuses. There was a frown on his brow and his lips were compressed.

Suddenly he spoke.

"Well," said Candon, "you've given me a name, what more have you to say?"

"Nothing," said George.

Candon turned, spat viciously over the rail and laughed, an odious sneering laugh that raised the bristles on Hank.

"It's easy to laugh," said Hank, "but it's no laughing matter to us. We've lost the *Wear Jack*, we've lost the boodle, we've lost our time, and we've been played a damn dirty trick, about as dirty as the trick the Chinks seem to have played on you."

Candon was not laughing now. He had turned to the starboard rail and was standing looking at the *Heart*. Tommie on the deck was clearly visible. She was looking at the *Wear Jack*; then she turned away and went below, as though to escape from the sight of him.

Candon gripped the rail tighter and heaved a deep breath. He turned to the others.

"So I've played you a dirty trick," said Candon. "Well, if I hadn't you'd have suspected me all the same, you'd never have said to yourselves maybe he didn't, let's ask him——"

"Ask him," said Hank. "What's the use, but I ask you now—Did you take that boat and go off to the *Wear Jack* for those automatics, leaving us there on that beach without pistols or means of fighting if the Mexicans came?"

"I did," said Candon, a curious light in his blue eyes.

"Did you sail off and leave us there?"

"I did."

"Well then, there's no use talking."

"Not a bit," said George.

"You finished?" asked Candon.

"Yep."

"Well then, that's Pat McGinnis' boat, he's been down to the bay, must have been or you wouldn't have collared it. What've you done with him?"

"That's nothing to you," said Hank.

"A minute," said George. "We've left him and his men there and we collared his boat, but we played the game he forced on us, and we played it straight."

"So you say," said Candon. "How'm I to know?"

"You suspect us!" fired Hank.

"And why not? You suspected me, the whole three of you jumped on me like this directly you came on board, never asked a question, not you, because you weren't true friends, hadn't the makin's of friendship in you, never asked for reasons."

Hank flushed. "Good Lord!" said he, "you mean to say you had a reason for leaving us like that?"

"No, I hadn't," replied the other, "but that's nothing. It's nothing if I'm the biggest blackguard on earth, as I intend to be. What's the good of being honest when you're written down a rogue out of hand the first traverse that seems suspicious—even if you are a rogue. Why, God bless my soul, them diamonds, you wouldn't trust them on the beach with me, you must take and shove them aboard the *Jack*."

"I never thought of you," said Hank. "I was thinking of the Mexicans coming down on us."

"Maybe," said Candon. "So you say, but how'm I to know." He spoke with extraordinary bitterness. To George the whole thing was beyond words, the evidence of a mentality bordering on the insane. Here was a man guilty of the betrayal of his companions, guilty of leaving them marooned on a hostile beach, yet not only unashamed but highly indignant that they should have suspected him and declared him guilty offhand. It was true there was something in what he said; they had taken his action as the action of a rogue almost from the first, but they could not have done otherwise.

He was determined to put this point right. "Look here," he said, "we might have thought you put off for some reason other than making away with that boodle, if you hadn't said you were going to leave us."

"I said I was going to stick in Mexico," replied Candon. "But there's no use in talking any more. Question is, what to do now. I can't stick here and I don't want to go on the *Heart*, unless I berth forward and help to work the ship. You can put me ashore somewhere."

"You'll have to berth with Jake," said Hank. "He's the fellow that was on the quay that night we put off and gave the show away to McGinnis."

"He'll do," said Candon, "I reckon he's good enough for me."

"Well, you'd better get your things then," said George.

They went down into the cabin one after the other, Candon leading.

The first things that struck Hank's eyes, were the automatic pistols lying on the tray shelf where he had seen them last.

Hank went to his bunk where he had hid the diamonds. The parcel was gone.

"I suppose the Chinks took the boodle as well as the boat," said he.

"That's so," replied Candon.

"Seems to me you didn't make much of a fight, seeing you had those pistols."

"I didn't make any fight at all."

Hank sniffed. George said nothing. They were busy now collecting their property. The Chinks had touched nothing but the diamonds. Hadn't time, most likely, to think of anything but escape from the wreck, and the chance of being found by some ship on the vessel they had helped Candon to run away with.

"What made you show them the diamonds?" asked Hank, as he stuffed Tommie's possessions into a bag.

"I didn't," said Candon.

"Then who told them?"

"The man who brought them on board."

"That was me. I said nothing."

He remembered how Tommie had put the things on and how the two Chinks had seen her. They had rowed him off with the package and might have given the news to the others. However, it didn't matter much and he was inclined for no more talk with B. C. He felt he had lowered himself already by speaking of the matter at all to the fellow.

Then they put the dunnage on deck and transshipped it in two journeys to the *Heart*. Tommie was on deck again when Candon came on board. She just nodded to him, and then turned to help getting the things down to the cabin. Candon's lot went into the foc'sle. Then he, Jake and George set to on the windlass, getting the anchor chain in.

It was the queerest and weirdest business, for B. C. showed neither shame nor irritation nor anger. A tremendous placidity seemed to have fallen upon him, almost a mild cheerfulness. He worked away and spoke to no one, he might have been an absolute stranger, a new hand just signed on.

When the *Heart* was under way, Hank and George picked watches. Hank had first call and picked Jake. George said nothing. Candon had fallen to him automatically.

Then Candon went down into the foc'sle to arrange his things and see after his bunk and with Hank at the wheel, the schooner lay again on her old course, the far-off crying of the gulls round Santander rock following them like the voice of mockery.

CHAPTER XXXVII

JAKE IS FIRED AGAIN

THEY had left Cancer far behind, they had rejected Hank's first idea of steering out towards Honolulu and then making aboard for 'Frisco, they were taking the shortest way possible home, shaving the Channel Islands and almost careless about being stopped. They wanted to finish the voyage as quickly as possible. Candon there in the foc'sle made his presence felt right through the ship. It was as though he had died and his ghost were haunting them. He never spoke unless in reply to orders. He seemed living in a world of his own, a silent secretive world where emotions were not. They began to appreciate the fact that they had shipped in San Francisco, not an ordinary sailor man with blue eyes, but a personality absolutely outside the ambit of ordinary experience.

"It's getting on my spine," said Hank one day, as he sat in the fusty cabin smoking with George. "The man seems gone dead, no shame or nothing, just as if he'd never seen us before; unless he gets an order, and then he jumps to it."

"It's got on T. C.'s spine, too," said George. "Damn him, she's not the same. I see her staring in front of her sometimes as if she was looking at ghosts. She never laughs and she's off her feed."

"He's worse than a cargo of skeletons," said Hank, "and I've noticed T. C. I'm not thinking any more of her, Bud, in that way, but it gets me to see her crumpled. What are women made of, anyhow? Seems to me if they once get gone on a man they go clean mushy for good—and such a man! Why, I heard Jake joshing him in the foc'sle only yesterday—Jake—and he took it like a lamb. Gets me."

He got up and took some little photographs from a locker. They had salved George's kodak and developer from the *Wear Jack*, and Hank, just before starting, had taken half a dozen snaps of the *Jack* lying piled on the rocks. He had done this for no sentimental reasons, but as evidence whereby Tyrebuck could collect his insurance money. He looked at them now with glowing satisfaction. They were the only bright spots in this new business.

"Well," said he, "there's one thing. I won't have to pay Tyrebuck his ten thousand. Luck's been playing pretty dirty tricks on us, but she's let up for once, unless she piles us same as she did the *Jack*."

Keeping as they were, well to outward of the longitude of Guadeloupe, there was little fear of them hitting anything except a derelict. They passed and were passed by vessels, tanks and great four-masters, battered by Cape Horn or making south to meet him. The traffic has increased now-a-days in the waters between Panama and San Francisco; it has decreased between Panama and the Horn, and is decreasing. The Horn, that frightful criminal standing there facing the ceaseless march of the mountainous waves, and countered by the canal, has come to recognise the hatred of man. Day by day the ships that pass him grow fewer, till a day may come when they cease, leaving him in loneliness forever.

On the day that they passed the latitude of Santa Catalina Island out of sight far to starboard, an incident occurred.

Hank had already noticed the attitude of Jake towards Candon. Jake had evidently been putting two and two together, and arriving at conclusions not far wrong. The attitude of the after-guard towards B. C. completed the matter.

On this day, Hank, coming up to relieve George at the wheel, found Tommie talking to George; at the same moment Jake rose from the foc'sle hatch to relieve Candon. Candon's back was turned to Jake who wished to pass him.

"Now then, you big stiff," cried Jake, "shift yourself, will you?"

Then the explosion came.

Candon wheeled. Next moment Jake, caught by the waistband, went flying over the port rail, tossed away like a rag doll; the next, Candon was after him; the next, the *Heart of Ireland*, answering to the helm, was turning and coming up into the wind with all her canvas thrashing.

"Over with the dinghy," cried George, giving the wheel to Tommie, and letting go the halyards.

Tommie, without a word, watched, as the two men got the dinghy afloat. Then she was alone.

She ran to the rail for a moment and saw away on the lifting swell, the heads of Candon and Jake close together, Candon evidently supporting the other and the boat making straight for them.

Ten minutes later the boat was back and Jake, half drowned, was being hauled on board, Candon helping. Then Candon took him down to the foc'sle to revive him. The *Heart* was put on her course again and the incident was closed.

Next day, Jake, subdued, went on with his work and Candon with his, absolutely as though nothing had happened.

The day after that, with the American coast showing to starboard and San Francisco not far ahead, Candon spoke to Hank.

"May I ask for the loan of your stylographic pen?" said Candon.

"Sure," said Hank. "Do you want some paper?"

"I was going to ask for some," said the other.

Hank went below and fetched up a wad of note paper, some envelopes and the pen.

"Thanks," said Candon, and went off to the foc'sle. It was his watch below.

CHAPTER XXXVIII

THE ANCHOR TAKES THE MUD

SOME days later towards noon, the *Heart of Ireland*, with the north-west wind and a flooding tide, was making to enter the Golden Gate.

It was a perfect day. Tamalpais, on the port bow, showed clear against a diamond-bright blue sky; astern lay the sea of adventure and romance, blue as when first sighted by Balboa.

Hank was at the wheel and feeling pretty nervous of the bar, when Candon, who had just come on deck, came aft.

"I'll take you in," said Candon. He took the spokes, and Hank, walking to the starboard rail, stood close to George watching the land.

Then they moved a bit more forward to talk.

"What's T. C. doing?" asked Hank.

"Down below," said George, "getting things together. She's not likely to come up till he's off."

"You've fixed things up with him?"

"Yep. We'll drop anchor off Tiburon, I'll row him ashore in the dinghy. Wouldn't take money. Says he's got twenty dollars and it's all he wants. Lord, Hank! I'd give twenty hundred dollars if this hadn't happened, twenty thousand, for I liked him. I did. What is it makes men run crooked who were built to run straight?"

"Search me," said Hank.

The *Heart* began to take the tumble of the bar. They thrashed through and then came the old familiar places, Line Point, the Presidio, the Bay, breezed up and showing the same old ships and traffic, the ferry boats running like pond insects, the junks, the steamers with rust-red funnels, the pleasure yachts, the oyster boats.

As they drew on to Tiburon, a white steam yacht passing in the distance sent the music of a band along the breeze. It was playing "Suwanee." Closer in now, Hank went below. Hank, for all his leathery old face, was far more emotional than George, and his mind, for all his will power, would keep jumping over the barrier of B. C.'s atrocious act to the old days when he had loved B. C. as a man and brother.

Tommie was in the after cabin and invisible, and Hank, alone, sat down at the table and leaned his arms on it, staring at the grains in the wood and listening. Leaning like this, suddenly a tear that seemed in an awful hurry raced down his right cheek; he did not know it. He was talking to himself, repeating the same words over and over again.

"Damn scoundrel. Damn scoundrel. Damn scoundrel."

Then, suddenly, the way fell off, a voice on deck gave an order, and the sound of the anchor chain rasped through the ship. The anchor was down.

Other sounds came that told him what was going on, then silence.

He came up. There was no one on deck but Jake chewing and spitting overside. Away on the water, making for the wharf, was the dinghy, George rowing, Candon in the stern. Hank stood watching for a moment, calling up in his mind the day when, talking to George in the cabin of the *Wear Jack*, Candon first came on board. He could see him plainly as he stood in the doorway, huge, friendly looking, with those eyes, the clear, blue, truthful eyes of a child. He called up all those discussions of an evening when George was ashore and Candon hiding from McGinnis and his men, those long talks covering the world and men and women—including Ella Wheeler Wilcox. The thing made him feel frightened as though the solid deck beneath his feet were threatened to dissolve. B. C. had been in earnest during those conversations, dead earnest, yet look what he had done. If that were so, how was he, Hank, to make sure he wasn't as bad as B. C.? Good one moment, bad the next? He tried to recall all the mean things he had ever done, going right back to his childhood. He couldn't remember anything in particular except nicking some apples off a stall. Then he gave up thinking, and came below, where he found Tommie who had finished putting things straight. She looked pale and pretty miserable and Hank's heart went out to her, so that he might have revealed what was in it only for his recollection of Zillah backed by Candon. Providence also helped, for at that moment, through the open ports, he heard a quick running launch checking her speed and coming washing alongside. A voice hailed Jake.

"It's the Port man," said Hank. He darted up to the companion way, looking over and saw the Port Authority man. It was old Captain Scudder, a friend.

"Hullo, Hank!" cried Scudder. "Lord bless my soul, where have you sprung from? Where's the old *Wear Jack*?"

"Come on board," said Hank, helping him up. "Come along down—this is better'n beans. Thought it might be some chap I didn't know."

"Got the Dutchman?" asked Scudder as he came down the companion way.

"Well, you might almost say I have," replied Hank, "but I'll tell you the yarn."

Tommie had retired into the after cabin and they sat down whilst Hank, knowing the man he was speaking to, gave his story, with big cuts but all essentials.

"So you see," finished Hank, "McGinnis is down and out, can't come back to 'Frisco with the fear of us on top of him. He was Vanderdecken practically speaking. But I've got some of his money and this old schooner to hand over to his wife if he's got one."

"Well, if you ask me he's got a widow, if I know anything of those Mexicans," replied Scudder. "Yes, he had a wife, she lives in Lincoln Street, and we'll fix it with her. Listen, there's a boat come alongside."

It was George returned. He came down and took a hand whilst they debated matters with Scudder.

"Take my advice," said the captain, "and keep your heads shut. You piled and lost the *Wear Jack* and came home in a schooner that happened along. Tell that to your friends. I'll smother the yarn as far as my side lies and I'll look after Jake. There is no use in stirring up trouble. Why, it might mean a dust-up with Mexico. Don't bother about being kidded at not bringing Vanderdecken home. He's half forgot, there's an election on—you know 'Frisco. As for that movie company and the show of theirs you bust up—Wallack and Jackson it was—there was a big story about it in the papers—but Wallack and Jackson is bust themselves. A week ago they went, with half a dozen others."

"Well, that's a comfort," said Hank, forgetting Tommie, and her means of livelihood.

Then Scudder heaved himself up and took his leave, and Tommie came out of the after cabin.

"Say," said Hank, suddenly remembering the importance of Scudder's news and recognising the gravity of it to her, "Old Scudder, the Port man has been here and we've fixed everything up all right, but he's brought bad news. Your show has bust."

"Which?" asked Tommie.

"Jackson and what's-his-name."

"I don't wonder," said Tommie, "it has been going a long time. Well, it doesn't matter to me, I've been careful and put by. I've thirty thousand dollars laid by with Aunt Coulthurst. She lives in Montgomery Street and I'm tired of the movies anyway. I want real life and I'm going to get it."

"How?" asked Hank.

"Ranch."

"Where?"

"Where I was born. Texas. There's air there, and life."

"Sure," said Hank.

"I'll buy a ranch and run it. It's a better life than being thrown out of windows for fools to look at or dropping from aëroplanes."

"Sure," said Hank.

"Well," said Tommie, taking her seat for a moment on a bunk side and speaking as if in a reverie, "I suppose this is the end of our trip. It's been queer, and we've had tight shaves but I wouldn't have missed it for earths. It's taught me more than I ever knew and it's made me have no fear in striking out for myself in life. I was never afraid of things, but I used to be frightened of life and what was to come the day after next, and I guess that's clean gone."

"What are you going to do now, when you get ashore?" asked George.

"I'm going to Aunt Coulthurst; 16, Montgomery Street is her address, and don't you forget it, and come and see us, won't you?"

"Sure," said Hank.

"Come Sunday. You'll love her and—and—" finished Miss Coulthurst, with a catch in her voice, "I want her to thank you, for you've both been very—very—good to me."

Hank seemed swallowing something.

"We'll come with pleasure," said George.

There was a pause, during which George took a letter from his pocket and gave it to Hank. It was a letter Candon had given him at parting; it had been written on the voyage with the stylograph pen he had borrowed and it was addressed to Hank Fisher.

"'Scuse me," said Hank, and as Tommie rose to get her hat before going, he opened the letter and began to read.

He hadn't been reading long when his jaw began to drop, he stopped dead and stared before him, took up the letter again, then handed it to George.

"That does me," said Hank. "Read it—read it out—read it."

Tommie stood by whilst George read out the letter. This is a verbatim copy:

"You called me a scoundrel. I am, maybe, but not the way you meant. Right away from the first you said to yourselves, the whole three of you, that this fellow Candon had let you down, gone off with the ship and boodle. You asked me had I gone aboard for those pistols, and I said I had. You asked me had I sailed off and left you and I said I had. You asked me had I any reason for going, meaning, in your left-handed way, was I a blackguard or not, and I said I hadn't. I hadn't. I was took.

"I'll tell you. When I left the beach that night and got the Chinks to row me aboard for those automatics, I found the cabin on board lit, the bunk bedding all pulled about and everything upside down and Charlie down there putting things to rights. I said to myself, that's Hank's work, the Chinks have nosed the diamonds and been on the search, and got them, to judge by the mess they've made. I saw it was serious but said nothing, went to the locker for the guns and whilst my back was turned, Charlie slipped on deck. The guns were there, the Chinks had been too busy to hunt for them. I took one of the automatics and saw it was loaded. As I was handling it, I heard the door of the cabin hatch shut and knew at once I was bottled and cursed myself for being such a fool and not getting on deck quicker. I remembered the galley hatch and made for it, nearly killing myself against the foc'sle bulkhead. The galley hatch was shut. I made back for the cabin and tried to burst the door. It was held like a rock by the bolts and something shoved against it. I thought of firing an automatic out of one of the ports for help, till I remembered you had no boat. If I'd once dreamed that you'd have suspected me, I'd have fired the lot, but I could not think that and it never entered my mind."

George paused for a moment.

"That shows you what jumping at conclusions too quickly, comes to. Here's the best fellow on earth, seems to me, and we—at least I did—yes, I did, I wrote him off as a scoundrel right from the beginning—almost."

"We didn't," cried Tommie. "I didn't, I know I felt there must be something that took him away. I never gave up hope till I saw you all standing on the deck of the *Wear Jack* and that you were scarcely speaking to him, and that he didn't seem to be explaining things—I don't know if I even quite gave up then—oh, dear!"

Her agitation made Hank blaze up.

"Why in the nation," he cried, "couldn't he have explained."

"You called him a scoundrel," said George. "He saw we'd marked him down without trial, and he was that sort."

"Which sort?"

"The sort that will kill you if you hit its pride, even if it has to kill itself. I expect that time in the foc's'le with Jake was pure hell's delight to him, feeling he was making us miserable and being miserable himself. I expect he's gloating at this present minute over us reading this letter and being unable to get at him to make things up. Gloating with pleasure, yet in hell all the time."

"Why, Bud," said Hank, "you're talking as if you knew the man's mind inside out."

"Maybe, I do," said Bud. "Maybe I'm not such a fool as I look, but I take him as a discontented man who's made a mess of his life, and nicking on him and calling him names like that just at that moment, finished the business."

Tommie nodded. All the same she guessed the case to be a bit more complicated than that.

"Go on reading," she said.

George went on.

"I sat down on one of the couches thinking what to do and I heard the Chinks pow-wowing away on deck. Talking maybe of how to get rid of me. Time went on and the clock went round to twelve, that's two hours after I boarded her, then Charlie came to the skylight and hailed me. He said they'd taken the ship and had got the stuff we were digging for. He asked me would I navigate her if they let me out. I told him to go to hell. He went off and time went on and then I heard them handling the halyards and getting in the hook. They didn't shout at their work, went silent as cats. Then I felt the ship under way.

"Morning came. I daren't sleep or they'd have been down on me, but I had food from the lazarette and there was water in the swinging bottle.

"Charlie came again that day to know if I would help work the ship. He said they meant to beach her on the Panama coast at a place they knew and offered me a share in the boodle. I told him I'd fire the ship first and he went away.

"That night, about three hours after dark as far as I could guess, for the clock had run down and I hadn't bothered to wind it, and they'd taken the chronometer with the charts on deck, a smash came and I knew the fools had piled her. I heard them shouting and pow-wowing. The sea was smooth and I knew they could easy get away if they didn't foul the boat in lowering her. They got her over all right and I heard them putting their dunnage in, grub and water, too, if they weren't crazy. Then I heard nothing more. They'd gone.

"The lamp was still alight. I'd put it out in the day time and lit up before dark; all the same, there wasn't much oil in her. So I set to on the cabin hatch working with my knife. I left off to get one of the automatics to see if I couldn't smash up the wood by firing, when, just taking it, I felt a draught of air blowing towards the skylight. I'd thought of getting out by the skylight, but the Chinks had thought of it too, and they'd overlaid it with ropes, but that draught blowing towards it gave me a jog and I made down along to the galley. The galley hatch was open.

"The Chinks must have opened it before running away, reckoning that if anything turned up and they were caught it would be lighter for them if they hadn't killed me.

"I got out on deck, couldn't see the boat. Then I opened the cabin hatch and let the air in.

"Then I had some grub and laid down and went asleep. I dreamt I heard a boat coming alongside. I tumbled out and came on deck and found my pals.

"You know the rest."

"BOB CANDON."

CHAPTER XXXIX

VANDERDECKEN

CANDON with his bundle under his arm walked from the stage where George had landed him to the ferry wharf. He did not intend staying at Tiburon, he wanted to lose himself, put himself beyond possible reach of Hank and George. He was waiting for the San Francisco ferry.

He felt uplifted, light-headed, full and satisfied with the knowledge that George Du Cane and the others would be reading his letter by now. He had revenged himself on himself, on society, and on his companions. Right from his first joining in with Hank and George, under everything had lain the fact that he was an outlaw, coupled with the fact that he had joined the *Wear Jack* through subterfuge. His confession at San Nicolas had seemingly cleared the slate, yet the fact remained; you cannot confess a fact away. He had been forgiven by Hank and Bud, and Tommie had declared her opinion that he would be all right with the Almighty when he'd prayed himself out of the hole he was in by hard work and the restoration of the jewels. Just so. Yet the fact remained that he had run crooked.

It had been like a grit in the eye. Sometimes he did not feel it, other times he did, but it had been there all the time.

It was his sense of inferiority always fretting his pride, his pride always fretful that had, perhaps, brought about the end of everything.

A lesser man or a greater man might have defended himself, explained or tried to explain.

He took his place in the ferry boat, crammed with the usual crowd. At it drew off from the wharf, he saw the *Heart of Ireland* as she lay at anchor. There was a figure on deck, it was Jake, the others were evidently down below. What were they saying, what were they doing? He watched the old schooner as she dimmed away into the distance across the breezy water, then he turned and looked at San Francisco standing before him in a blaze of light, the Palace Hotel, the hills veined with streets, the docks and shipping, all so vast, so indifferent, brilliant, self-possessed and cruel.

Nature in her worst moods has made nothing more daunting than a city. Candon had never felt this as he felt it now. The *Wear Jack* had been a home and he and his companions almost a family. In all the city he had not a friend. That is the worst of a sailor's life; unless he rises to the command of a ship and keeps it, the end of each voyage often means a break-up and separation from the men he sails with and the best friends part never to meet again. The sailor has no time ashore to make friends and the friends he makes at sea he loses.

Candon landed at the wharf and made for Essex Street where he had put up before. No. 12 was the house, an humble enough place, but clean and respectable, kept by a widow whose husband had been captain of one of the Oakland ferry boats.

He obtained a room, left his bundle and started out making up town. He had no object in view. In the old days he would most likely have drifted into a tavern, met companions and maybe friends under the freemasonry of drink; but those days are done with. Drink he could have got, poison, swallowed in a corner at five or ten times the price of the old stuff, but, though several touts spoke to him, recognising a man from the sea, he turned them down. Passing from street to street without caring where he went, the fact of his own isolation was borne in on him by every sight and sound. All these people had businesses, friends, acquaintances. He had none. If he were to drop dead not a soul would care.

He found himself amongst the sharp-faced hustling crowd of Market Street and drifted with it, scarcely seeing it, looking in at shop windows but scarcely noticing the goods. He was not walking alone now; the wraiths of Hank and George and Tommie were with him, walking on either side of him, and now in some extraordinary way his anger and enmity against them, against himself and against circumstances had faded. It was as though they were dead.

The loneliness of the great city, the very atmosphere of it had seized upon him, cut him off from those past few brilliant weeks of adventure and stress. He could no longer feel as he felt then. He tried, remembering how they had pre-judged him, to work up his feelings of only a few hours ago, but the old anger would not come. He had left it behind him on the *Heart of Ireland* or, maybe, on the ferry boat. Anger would not come, because the way was barred by a new-found sense of reason that kept saying to him, "Well, suppose they did? Look at the facts—they made a mistake—you were furious because you were innocent, but were you made of glass so that they could see your innocence? Not you; why you were Vanderdecken. You had already done a shady trick by getting on board the *Wear Jack* under that contract; you were no white lamb. Facts were against you and you were too proud to explain—that's the truth—and you had a grudge against everything. Well there it is and no more to be said."

He went into a picture house and sat for ten minutes and came out again and had some food.

It was evening now and the lamps were springing alight. He wandered down towards the docks, Hank, Bud and Tommie still clinging to him, and Reason, refreshed with a porter-house steak, clearing her throat to say something. Then in Tallis Street where the crimps abide, she said it.

"Swab!" Then she began to rub it in. "You wrote that letter. Every line you wrote, down there in the foc'sle of the *Heart*, was pure joy. You said to yourself, 'When they read this they will suffer.' That's what you said and what you felt. You didn't write to explain, you wrote to hit."

That was the truth.

They were the best people he had ever met and he had wounded them all he could. Done all he could to make them feel mean and small.

If they had not been the best people, the letter would have had no effect; if he had not loved them, the odious pleasure of writing it would not have been there. If he had not loved them, he would not have struck them, struck them with the feverish anger of the child that breaks and destroys the thing it cares for.

He walked on, making towards the water side, reviewing himself and his futilities.

Impulse and a volcanic nature had been his ruin right along from the first—and pride. And the devil of it was his impulse had always been—or nearly always—towards the good. Why, look away back to the time when he commanded a ship and had been fired for a volcanic letter to the owners for supplying his crew with "grub that a dog wouldn't eat." And he had chucked a good chance to go and fight in a war that had nothing to do with him, just because the Lusitania had been torpedoed. Look at the McGinnis business. Look at everything.

A man rarely sees himself in the glass of mind. When he does the image is rarely quite true. Candon saw a reflection uglier than the reality. At all events it was a good thing that he saw it. Then he went home and tried to sleep and could not.

At ten o'clock next morning, he found himself in Pacific Avenue, asking his way. At five minutes past ten, he was coming up the steps of a residence with Purbeckian marble pillars to the door-way.

He rang and Farintosh opened. Farintosh did not know if Mr. du Cane were in; he would see. He returned in a minute and ushered Candon into a library where Bud, in his shirt sleeves, was re-arranging some books. Bud had a pipe in his mouth.

Farintosh shut the door and the two men were left alone.

"Sit down," said Bud. There was no warmth in his tone. He seemed a different man from the Bud of the *Wear Jack*, older, more serious. Old Harley du Cane with his rose in his coat and his air of a *flaneur*, could sometimes crystallize into awful and icy seriousness, the man of pleasure suddenly becoming the man of affairs, cold, logical with something of the touch of the judge.

"I've come to say I haven't treated you people well," said Candon. "I'll never see you again, so I wanted just to say that. I couldn't sit down under it any longer. Couldn't sleep to-night without saying what I wanted to say. I shouldn't have given up that letter."

"You shouldn't," said Bud. He was standing with his back to the fireplace now, with his pipe in his mouth. "I'm not wanting to rub it in, but you've crumpled Tommie up. Steady on, and let me talk. I'm the man you ought to have a grouch against, for when the *Wear Jack* went off, I was the first to say you'd taken your hook. I had to kick Hank to make him believe. Hank's a good sort, much better than me, much better than you, much better than any of us. He believed in you, so did Tommie. Well, now, see here, B. C., I'm not going to apologise to you for being mistaken and for writing you down worse than you were, for the facts were all dead against you, and it was no pleasure to me to think you'd hooked it. It cut me bad. Let's forget it and come to the point. I guess the Almighty sent you here to-night for me to deal with and I'm going to deal with you straight. One moment."

He left the room, and Candon heard him calling for Farintosh and giving some directions, then he returned, took his place on the hearth rug and went on.

"Yes, I guess he did. What are your plans?"

"Foc'sle."

"Yes, the foc'sle of some wind-jammer, fine time and fine prospects. Well, I've made different plans for you, made them long ago, dropped them when that beastly business happened, but I've picked them up again, right now."

"I reckon a dive into the harbour would be the best plan for me," said Candon. He was seated with his arms folded, wilted, miserable. He was thinking of Tommie and what Bud had said about her.

"It would," said Bud, "if you are an ass and don't fall in with what I want to do."

"Yes?"

"You've got to take my money, work and pay me back—fruit farm or ranch. Quit the sea, the sea's no use to you, B. C., and I tell you that straight."

"It's good of you," said the other shaking his head. "It's darn good of you, Bud du Cane—you said that before. It's not my pride. I reckon I've no pride left, but where's the good? I guess I'm too far gone for any man to help me. I've lost clutch of myself in the last two days. I tell you it's as if I'd been boiled and my back-bone taken out of me. I'm changed, that's a fact. All my life I've never lost confidence in myself till now. You remember how I took the *Wear Jack* out of harbour that night? I could no more do that now than I could fly—I've lost confidence in myself."

"And maybe a good thing, too," said George.

"I don't know," said Candon, "maybe it's good or bad, but there's the fact. A while ago I was a man who could lead things, now I feel all I want is to take orders."

"Good," said George, "and now you're talking like a man. What do you think a man is, anyway? Why, till he learns to take orders, he hasn't got the makings of a man in him. And now I'm going to give you your orders, B. C. You've got to make a home for a girl that cares for you. She's got money enough of her own, but you can't take a woman's money, but you can take mine as a loan, and if you don't make good, why you aren't the man I think you are."

"Cares for me?" said Candon, as though he were a bit deaf and not sure that he had caught the other's words.

"Yes, unless I have no sense or judgment left. But she'll tell you herself in a minute. I've sent for her."

He left the room.

Candon got up and walked to and fro for a long time, his hands behind his back. Then he lifted up his chin and gazed before him with those clear eyes trained to look over vast distances.

The manhood had come back to him with the call to a greater adventure than any he had ever undertaken.

He heard an automobile drawing up in the street—voices. Then the door opened and Tommie stood before him. It closed, leaving them alone.

That is the story of Vanderdecken as told to me by Hank Fisher. The story of a man of temperament saved from himself by a woman. I met George du Cane at Pasadena a little while ago and he corroborated the tale giving me a few extra details left out by Hank. George said Tyrebuck collected his insurance all right on the *Wear Jack*, also that McGinnis and his crowd managed to escape from the Mexicans, and, making down the coast, were rescued by a tanker which had put into Santa Clara Bay owing to a defect in her machinery. They returned to San Francisco, but made no trouble, or only with Mrs. McGinnis, who had sold the *Heart of Ireland* and invested the money in a laundry, thinking McGinnis dead.

Hank married his girl quite recently and Candon and Tommie are happy, but the thing uppermost in George's mind in connection with this business was the treasure.

He took an old press cutting from his pocket book and showed it to me. It gave news of a boatful of dead Chinamen found and sunk by the British cruiser *Hesperia* down by the Galapagos Islands.

"They'd have sunk it maybe with a shell," said George; "it would have given them fine target practice for one of their small guns and they'd never have overhauled it for jewelry.

"It's a hundred to one it was the boat of the *Wear Jack*. The *Wear Jack's* whaler had no name on it, and it's just the position they'd have been in by drifting. You see the Kiro Shiwo would have brought them down past the line and then they'd have met Humboldt's current; that would have pushed them back, and there they'd have been drifting and messing about when the *Hesperia* came along. Anyhow," finished George, "whatever's become of those jewels, they've never been seen since, and it's my opinion, they'll never be seen again."

THE END.

Milton Keynes UK
Ingram Content Group UK Ltd.
UKHW030740071024
449371UK00006B/679